a Daily Catholic
moment

TEN MINUTES A DAY ALONE WITH GOD

COMPILED BY PETER CELANO

WITH DAILY INSPIRATIONS FROM THE SAINTS:
Athanasius, Catherine of Siena, Francis of Assisi,
John Chrysostom, John of the Cross, John Henry Cardinal Newman,
Teresa of Avila, and Thérèse of Lisieux,

**AS WELL AS GREAT WRITERS, POETS, AND THEOLOGIANS
PAST AND PRESENT:**
Br. Benet Tvedten OSB, Enzo Bianchi, G. K. Chesterton, Dorothy
Day, Thomas Groome, Fr. Albert Haase OFM, Sr. Bridget Haase OSU,
Thomas Merton OCSO, Henri J. M. Nouwen, Thomas J. Scirghi SJ,
Bonnie Thurston, Br. Paul Quenon OCSO, Timothy Verdon,
and the Desert Fathers and Mothers.

PARACLETE PRESS
BREWSTER, MASSACHUSETTS

2014 First printing

A Daily Catholic Moment: Ten Minutes a Day Alone With God

Copyright © 2014 by Paraclete Press, Inc.

ISBN 978-1-61261-575-2

Library of Congress Cataloging-in-Publication Data
A daily Catholic moment : ten minutes a day alone with God / compiled by Peter Celano.
    pages cm
  ISBN 978-1-61261-575-2 (trade pbk.)
  1. Devotional calendars—Catholic Church. 2. Catholic Church—Prayers and devotions.
I. Celano, Peter, compiler.
  BX2170.C56D35 2014
  242'.2—dc23   2014029005
10 9 8 7 6 5 4 3 2 1

Published by Paraclete Press
Brewster, Massachusetts
www.paracletepress.com

Printed in the United States of America

"Since we have made up our minds to devote this
brief period of time to Him . . .
let us give it to Him freely with our minds
unoccupied by other things.
We should make up our minds not to take
back the time we have committed
to Him, no matter what kinds of trials
or annoyances we suffer.
Let me realize that this time is being lent to me,
and it is not my own.
I can rightly be called to account for this
time if I am not prepared to devote it
entirely to God."

—St. Teresa of Avila

Contents

January

JANUARY 1

$\mathcal{T}$oday is the Solemnity of Mary, the Mother of God

"Oh, beloved Mother, with what gratitude do I sing of the mercies of the Lord! Wasn't I, according to these words of Wisdom, 'taken away, lest wickedness should alter my understanding, or deceit beguile my soul' [cf. Wis. 4:11]? The Blessed Virgin also was watching over [me] her little flower, and not wanting her to be faded by contact with the things of the earth, she withdrew her onto her mountain before she had fully opened." —St. Thérèse of Lisieux

Hail Mary, full of grace, the Lord is with thee; blessed are thou among women, and blessed is the fruit of thy womb, Jesus. Holy Mary, Mother of God, pray for us sinners, now and at the hour of our death. Amen.

JANUARY 2

$\mathcal{B}$ut above all bless your Maker,
who fills you with his good gifts.
—Sirach 32:13 (NRSV)

"Humble and continuous prayer, founded on knowledge of one-self and of God, is the best way for any creature to receive a taste of the truth. Following the footprints of Christ crucified, and through humble and unceasing prayer, the soul is united with God."—St. Catherine of Siena

Bring me close to You today, Lord, my Creator, my Savior.

JANUARY 3

$\mathscr{L}$ittle children, let us love, not in word or speech,
but in truth and action.
—1 John 3:18 (NRSV)

"[St. Francis of Assisi] was a Lover. He was a lover of God and he was really and truly a lover of men; possibly a much rarer mystical vocation. A lover of men is very nearly the opposite of a philanthropist; indeed the pedantry of the Greek word carries something like a satire on itself. A philanthropist may be said to love anthropoids. But as St. Francis did not love humanity but men, so he did not love Christianity but Christ."
—G. K. Chesterton

**Show me who to love today, Lord. Remind me
to see You in the faces of people I meet.**

JANUARY 4

$\mathscr{I}$f I speak in the tongues of mortals and of angels,
but do not have love, I am a noisy gong
or a clanging cymbal.
—1 Corinthians 13:1 (NRSV)

"Can you see what point [St. Paul] is making when he begins by exalting the gift, and then to what extent afterward he lowers and casts it down? For he doesn't simply say, 'I am nothing,' but instead he says, 'I am a noisy gong or a clanging cymbal,' a senseless and inanimate thing. What does he mean by a clanging cymbal? He emits a sound, but at random and in vain, and for no good purpose. Beautiful speech that profits nothing also counts you as one giving impertinent trouble, an annoying and even wearisome kind of person. Do you see how a person who is void of love is similar to things that are inanimate and senseless?" —St. John Chrysostom

Show me how to love with Your love, today, Lord.

JANUARY 5

[*Jesus said,*] "[I]f you have faith the size of a mustard seed, you will say to this mountain, 'Move from here to there,' and it will move; and nothing will be impossible for you."
—Matthew 17:20b–21 (NRSV)

"You should believe everything you hear about Antony. He performed extraordinary works, and you have until now only heard about the least remarkable ones. For even I do not know everything about him, and I will not be able to tell you accurately everything about his exceptional character." —St. Athanasius

God, make my life a blessing to people today.

[*Jesus said*,] "[W]henever you pray, go into your room and shut the door and pray to your Father who is in secret."

—Matthew 6:6a (NRSV)

During a time of intense persecution of Christians, "St. Paul the First Hermit fled to the mountainous regions of the desert . . . making a virtue of necessity. He came at last to a rocky mountain, at the foot of which was a small cave. Removing the stone that blocked the cave's entrance, he began to explore more eagerly. Inside, he found a large room, open to the sky and covered by the spreading branches of a palm tree. . . . Paul fell in love with the dwelling as if God had offered it to him. He spent the rest of his life there in prayer and solitude. The palm tree provided him with food and clothing. In case anyone should think this impossible, I call Jesus and the holy angels to witness that in some parts of the desert I have seen monks, one enclosed for thirty years, living on barley bread and muddy water. Another monk survived in an old well, living on five dried figs a day. These things will appear incredible only to those who do not believe that everything is possible for those who believe."

—St. Jerome

**I will find my own "mountain" or "cave" this year,
as I recommit myself to a life of prayer.**

JANUARY 7

[*Jesus said,*] "[W]hoever does not receive the kingdom of God as a little child will never enter it."
—Luke 18:17 (NRSV)

"I understood that Our Lord's love is revealed as well in the simplest soul who doesn't resist His grace in anything, as in the most sublime of souls. In fact, since the essence of love is to bring oneself low, if every soul were like the souls of the holy Doctors who have shed light on the Church through the clarity of their doctrine, it seems that God wouldn't come down low enough by coming only as far as their great hearts. But He created the child who doesn't know anything and only cries weakly."
—St. Thérèse of Lisieux

Some days I feel like a theologian, Lord. Other days, I'm a little child. Thanks for loving me either way.

JANUARY 8

[*Jesus said,*] "[D]o not worry about your life. . . . [C]an any of you by worrying add a single hour to your span of life?"
—Matthew 6:25a, 27 (NRSV)

"I have the fewest worries when I possess least, and the Lord knows that I am more afflicted when I have an excess of anything than when I have a lack of anything. I am not sure if it's the Lord's doing, but I have noticed that He provides for us immediately." —St. Teresa of Avila

I don't want to worry about money, Lord.
I am renewing my trust in You.

═ JANUARY 9 ═

And the Word became flesh and lived among us,
and we have seen his glory, the glory as of a father's
only son, full of grace and truth.
—John 1:14 (NRSV)

St. Catherine of Siena eagerly looked forward "to the morning's arrival in order to hear Mass." She once reflected: "In such communion, the soul binds itself firmly to God, and knows better His truth, since the soul is then in God and God in the soul."

I rush to meet You today, Lord.

═ JANUARY 10 ═

Little children, you are from God . . . [and] the one who is
in you is greater than the one who is in the world.
—1 John 4:4 (NRSV)

St. Catherine of Siena continues her reflection on preparing for the Mass, talking about herself in the third person: "When the hour of Mass arrived in the morning—it was the feast day of Mary—she anxiously sought her usual place. From a deep knowledge of herself and with a feeling of holy justice, she was ashamed of her own imperfection, for it seemed to be the cause of all the world's evils. In this knowledge, she cleansed the stains covering her guilty soul, saying, 'Eternal Father, I accuse myself before You, so that You may punish me for my sins in this life. Since my sins cause my neighbor to suffer, I beg You, in Your mercy, to punish me for them.'"

You alone are the source of my strength, my joy, my justice.

══ JANUARY 11 ══

*G*ive ear to my prayer, O God; do not hide
yourself from my supplication.
—Psalm 55:1 (NRSV)

"I need far greater knowledge and experience than I have to describe this dark night through which the soul passes in order to reach the divine light of the perfect union of God's love. This darkness and these spiritual and temporal trials through which happy souls pass in order to be able to reach this high state of perfection are so numerous and so profound that human knowledge is not fully capable of describing them. The only persons who can describe this dark night are the ones who experience it, and even they cannot describe it accurately."
—St. John of the Cross

There are some things I can say only to You, God.

JANUARY 12

We are fools for the sake of Christ, but you are wise in
Christ. We are weak, but you are strong. You are held in
honor, but we in disrepute.
—1 Corinthians 4:10 (NRSV)

"Some might call him a madman, but he was the very reverse of
a dreamer. Nobody would be likely to call him a man of business;
but he was very emphatically a man of action. In some of his
early experiments he was rather too much of a man of action;
he acted too soon and was too practical to be prudent. But at
every turn of his extraordinary career we shall find him flinging
himself around corners in the most unexpected fashion, as when
he flew through the streets after the beggar." —G. K. Chesterton,
writing about St. Francis of Assisi

**Make me impetuous today, Lord. Let's call it courage.
Take me out of my comfort zone to serve You.**

JANUARY 13

Indeed the word of God is living and active, sharper
than any two-edged sword, piercing until it divides soul
from spirit, joints from marrow; it is able to judge the
thoughts and intentions of the heart.
—Hebrews 4:12 (NRSV)

"When [St. Antony] and his little sister were left completely on their own after their parents died (Antony was around eighteen years old), he took good care of his house and his sister. Before six months had passed, though, he was on his way to church one day when he thought about how the apostles had rejected everything to follow the Savior. He thought about how the early Christians had sold their possessions and laid the proceeds at the apostles' feet to distribute to the needy. What great hope was stored up for those people in heaven! As he was thinking about these things, Antony entered the church [and] he heard this Gospel being read: "If you wish to be perfect, go, sell your possessions and give the money to the poor, and you will have treasure in heaven; then come, follow me" (Matt. 19:21). When he heard this, Antony applied the Lord's commandment to himself, believing that because of divine inspiration he had first remembered the incident and that this Scripture was being read aloud for his sake. He immediately went home and sold the possessions he owned." —St. Athanasius

Show me, Holy Spirit, in some small way, how to apply your Holy Scriptures to my life.

══ JANUARY 14 ══

ℬe merciful to me, O God, be merciful to me, for in you my soul takes refuge . . . until the destroying storms pass by.
    —Psalm 57:1 (NRSV)

As he concludes the short *Life* of St. Paul the First Hermit, St. Jerome writes: "I would like to ask the wealthy, 'What did this old man ever lack, naked as he was? You drink from jeweled cups, but he was satisfied with the cupped hands that nature had given him. . . . He was clothed with Christ despite his nakedness. You who are dressed in silks have lost the garment of Christ. Paul, who lies covered in the vilest dust, will rise again in glory. . . . I beg you, whoever you are, to remember the sinner Jerome. If the Lord would grant him his wish, he would rather choose Paul's tunic, and his rewards, than the purple robes of kings, and their punishments.'"

Dear God, guide me today as I try to live only for what matters in eternity.

═══ JANUARY 15 ═══

*F*or your immortal spirit is in all things. Therefore you
correct little by little those who trespass, and you remind and
warn them of the things through which they sin, so that they
may . . . put their trust in you, O Lord.
—Wisdom 12:1–2 (NRSV)

"You will probably laugh at me and say how obvious such things are. But, until I closed my eyes to the vanities of this world, I did not see or understand who lived within my soul or what my soul deserved. If I had understood then, as I now do, how this great King lives within this palace of my soul, I would not have left

Him alone so much. I would have stayed with Him and not let His house get so dirty. It is wonderful that He whose greatness could fill a thousand worlds should confine Himself to so small a space, just as He was pleased to inhabit His most holy Mother's womb. As our Lord, He has perfect freedom, and because He loves us, He fashions Himself to our measure." —St. Teresa of Avila

I will not neglect You, today, Lord. Help me be mindful of Your presence in my life.

═══ JANUARY 16 ═══

The LORD, your God, is in your midst, a warrior who gives victory; he will rejoice over you with gladness, he will renew you in his love; he will exult over you with loud singing.
—Zephaniah 3:17 (NRSV)

"By bringing Himself low in this way, God shows His infinite greatness. Just as the sun shines at the same time on the tall cedars and on each little flower as if it were the only one on earth, in the same way our Lord is concerned particularly for every soul as if there were none other like it." —St. Thérèse of Lisieux

I love how You love me!

JANUARY 17

*T*oday is the Feast Day of St. Antony the Great

St. Antony taught: "Let Christians care for nothing that they cannot take away with them. We ought rather to seek after that which will lead us to heaven, namely wisdom, chastity, justice, virtue, an ever-watchful mind, care of the poor, firm faith in Christ, a mind that can control anger, and hospitality. Striving after these things, we shall prepare for ourselves a dwelling in the land of the peaceful, as it says in the Gospel." —As recorded by St. Athanasius

What in the world am I clinging to, God?

JANUARY 18

"*B*e still, and know that I am God."
—Psalm 46:10a (NIV)

"[I]n practice . . . there is only one vocation. Whether you teach or live in the cloister or nurse the sick, whether you are in religion or out of it, married or single, no matter who you are or what you are, you are called to the summit of perfection: you are called to a deep interior life perhaps even to mystical prayer, and to pass the fruits of your contemplation on to others. And if you cannot do so by word, then by example." —Thomas Merton OCSO

I want to know You today.

JANUARY 19

*I*f we say that we have fellowship with him while we are walking in darkness, we lie and do not do what is true; but if we walk in the light as he himself is in the light, we have fellowship with one another, and the blood of Jesus his Son cleanses us from all sin.
—1 John 1:6–7 (NRSV)

St. Catherine of Siena recalled the words of Christ: "Forgiveness comes, then, through the soul's desire to be united to Me, the infinite Good, according to the measure of love attained by the recipient's desire and prayer. A person receives as much of My goodness as he gives to Me."

I want to walk in Your light today.

JANUARY 20

I cry to God Most High, to God who fulfills his purpose for me.
—Psalm 57:2 (NRSV)

"[St. Antony] obeyed [all of the holy men of the desert] whom he visited. Eager to learn, he assimilated their various individual gifts. He imitated the self-restraint of one; the cheerfulness of another. He emulated the gentleness of one; the nocturnal devotions of another; and the dedication in reading of yet another. He admired one who fasted and another who slept on the bare ground; praising the endurance of the former and the compassion of the latter. He kept in mind the love they all showed one another, and he returned to his own place refreshed by every aspect of their virtues." —St. Athanasius

**Focus me, Lord, on imitating the Christian virtue
of someone whom I know and respect.**

═══ JANUARY 21 ═══

*B*e firm, steadfast, always fully devoted to the work of the
Lord, knowing that in the Lord your labor is not in vain.
—1 Corinthians 15:58 (NAB)

"When the holy father Antony lived in the desert, he was overcome with many sinful thoughts. He said to God, 'Lord, I want to be saved, but these thoughts will not leave me alone. What can I do in my sickness? How can I be saved?' A short while later, when he got up to go out, Antony saw a man like himself sitting at his work, getting up from his work to pray, then sitting down to work again, and getting up again to pray. It was an angel of the Lord sent to correct and reassure him. He heard the angel saying to him: 'Do this, and you will be saved.' When he heard these words, Antony was filled with joy and courage. He did this, and he was saved." —*The Wisdom of the Desert Fathers and Mothers*

I will stop and pray today whenever temptations come my way.

JANUARY 22

[Jesus said,] "Take care not to perform righteous deeds in order that people may see them; otherwise, you will have no recompense from your heavenly Father."
—Matthew 6:1 (NAB)

"A poor person is seldom honored by the world, no matter how worthy of honor he might be. The world will more likely despise this person than honor him. A different kind of honor, to which no one can object, comes with true poverty. If one embraces poverty solely for God's sake, only God has to be pleased. A person who does not need anyone has many friends; I have found this to be true from my own experience." —St. Teresa of Avila

You are the friend I want, Lord. You are the only one I hope to impress.

JANUARY 23

The LORD is my shepherd, I shall not want.
He makes me lie down in green pastures;
he leads me beside still waters;
he restores my soul.
He leads me in right paths
for his name's sake.

Even though I walk through the darkest valley,
I fear no evil;
for you are with me;
your rod and your staff—
they comfort me.
—Psalm 23:1–4 (NRSV)

"I find myself at a point in my life when I can take a look back at the past. My soul has matured in the crucible of outward and inward trials. Now, like a flower strengthened by the storm, I lift my head, and I see that the words of the twenty-third psalm are coming true in me." —St. Thérèse of Lisieux

You are my Shepherd, Lord. Thanks for caring for me.

═══ JANUARY 24 ═══

*H*e has shown you, O mortal, what is good. And what does the Lord require of you? To act justly and to love mercy and to walk humbly with your God.
—Micah 6:8 (NIV)

"Let our houses be small and poor in every way. Let us be like our King, who had no house except the porch in Bethlehem where He was born and the cross on which He died. These were houses where little comfort could be found. Those who build large houses no doubt have good reasons for doing so; they are moved by various holy intentions. But any corner is sufficient. . . . God preserve us from building a large ornate convent with a lot of buildings. Always remember that these things will fall down on the Day of Judgment, and who knows how soon that will be?" —St. Teresa of Avila

Help me focus on what matters, and to put aside what doesn't.

═ JANUARY 25 ═

And now, little children, abide in him, so that when
he is revealed we may have confidence and not be
put to shame before him at his coming.
—1 John 2:28 (NRSV)

"Some work hard, yet make no progress. Others seek profit in what is not profitable. Still others are disturbed and make no progress precisely because of the favors that God grants so that they may make progress. Yet there are others who make great progress by remaining at rest and in quietness. There are many other things on this road that come to those who follow it—joys and afflictions and hopes and grief. Some come from the spirit of perfection and others from imperfection."
—St. John of the Cross

Show me, Christ, how to make progress in the spiritual life, today.

$\mathcal{P}$ut on then, as God's chosen ones, holy and beloved,
compassionate hearts, kindness, humility, meekness, and
patience, bearing with one another and, if one has a complaint
against another, forgiving each other; as the Lord has forgiven
you, so you also must forgive. And above all these put on love,
which binds everything together in perfect harmony.
—Colossians 3:12–14 (ESV)

Christ spoke to St. Catherine of Siena: "You achieve every virtue
and every defect by means of your neighbor. Those who hate
Me, therefore, injure their neighbor and therefore themselves,
who are their own chief neighbors. This injury is both general
and particular. It is general, because you are obliged to love
your neighbor as yourself. Because you love your neighbor, you
should help him spiritually, through prayer and by counseling
him with words. Assist him spiritually and temporally with your
good will, according to his needs."

I am part of Your great, compassionate Church.

$\mathcal{E}$ver since the creation of the world his eternal power and
divine nature, invisible though they are, have been understood
and seen through the things he has made.
—Romans 1:20a (NRSV)

"[T]he whole philosophy of St. Francis revolved around the idea of a new supernatural light on natural things, which meant the ultimate recovery not the ultimate refusal of natural things."
—G. K. Chesterton, writing about St. Francis of Assisi

Help me discern when and how to show disdain for "the things of the world," and when to praise what is truly You.

═══ JANUARY 28 ═══

No temptation has overtaken you that is not common to man. God is faithful, and he will not let you be tempted beyond your ability, but with the temptation he will also provide the way of escape, that you may be able to endure it.
—1 Corinthians 10:13 (ESV)

"While Antony was busy with doing all these things that caused so many to love him, the devil, who could not bear to see a young man with such outstanding virtues, began to attack him. First, he tried to drag Antony away from the life to which he had committed himself. He made Antony remember his wealth . . . and his family's social status. The devil tried to stimulate in Antony a desire for material things, the short-lived honors of this world, the pleasures of different kinds of food, and many other attractions that belong to an indulgent life. He reminded Antony of the great difficulty in obtaining the life of virtue. He also reminded him of the body's weakness. He created great confusion in Antony's thoughts, hoping to call him back from his intentions." —St. Athanasius

Give me the courage and patience of saints today, O Lord!

JANUARY 29

*F*or my thoughts are not your thoughts, neither are your
ways my ways, declares the LORD. For as the heavens are
higher than the earth, so are my ways higher than your
ways and my thoughts than your thoughts.
—Isaiah 55:8–9 (ESV)

"When Antony thought about the depth of God's judgments, he
asked, 'Lord, how is it that some die when they are young, while
others drag on to extreme old age? Why are there those who
are poor and those who are rich? Why do wicked men prosper,
and why are the just in need?' He heard a voice answering him,
"Antony, keep your attention on yourself; these things happen
according to God's judgment, and it is not to your advantage to
know anything about them.'"
—*The Wisdom of the Desert Fathers and Mothers*

**Quiet the questions in my heart, O Lord, that
keep me from being close to You.**

JANUARY 30

*P*ut on then, as God's chosen ones, holy and beloved,
compassionate hearts, kindness, humility,
meekness, and patience.
—Colossians 3:12 (ESV)

"It seems to me that if a little flower could talk, it would tell simply what God has done for it, without trying to hide its blessings. Under the pretext of a false humility it wouldn't say that it is unsightly and lacking in perfume, that the sun has taken away its beauty and its stem has been broken, while it recognizes just the opposite in itself." —St. Thérèse of Lisieux

I will praise You today, God, with my life and my words.

=== JANUARY 31 ===

[Jesus said,] "[U]nless you turn and become like children, you will not enter the kingdom of heaven. Whoever humbles himself like this child is the greatest in the kingdom of heaven."
—Matthew 18:3b–4 (NAB)

"You have asked me to say something to you about prayer. Before I speak about the interior life, that is, about prayer, I will speak of certain things that those walking along the way of prayer must practice. These things are so necessary that even people who are not greatly interested in contemplation can advance a long way in the Lord's service. However, unless they have these things they cannot possibly be great contemplatives, and if they think they are, they are mistaken. May the Lord help me in this task and teach me what I need to say, so it may be to His glory. . . . One of these is love for each other. The second is detachment from all created things. The third, true humility, is the most important of these and embraces all the rest." —St. Teresa of Avila

Give me love, detachment, and humility, so that I may pray.

February

After Jesus had finished instructing his twelve disciples,
he went on from there to teach and preach in the towns of
Galilee. When John, who was in prison, heard about the
deeds of the Messiah, he sent his disciples to ask him,
"Are you the one who was to come, or should we expect
someone else?" Jesus replied, "Go back and report to John
what you hear and see: The blind receive sight, the lame walk,
those who have leprosy are cleansed, the deaf hear, the dead are
raised, and the good news is proclaimed to the poor. Blessed is
anyone who does not stumble on account of me."
As John's disciples were leaving, Jesus began to speak to the
crowd about John: "What did you go out into the wilderness
to see? A reed swayed by the wind?"
—Matthew 11:1–7 (NIV)

"There are three reasons for which the soul's journey to union
with God is called night. The first has to do with the soul's starting point. It must gradually deprive itself of desire for all worldly
things by denying these things to itself. Such denial and depriva-
tion are night to the human senses. The second reason has to do
with the road along which the soul must travel to this union, that
is, faith, which also is as dark as night to the understanding. The
third has to do with the point to which it travels—that is, God,
who is equally a dark night to the soul in this life. The soul must
pass through these dark nights so that it may come to divine
union with God." —St. John of the Cross

Lord, help me to see.

FEBRUARY 2

Love is patient, love is kind. . . . Love never fails.
—1 Corinthians 13:4a, 8a (NAB)

St. Catherine of Siena heard God say to her: "A person who does not love does not help his neighbor, and thus harms himself. He cuts himself off from grace, and harms his neighbor by depriving him of the benefit of the prayers and sweet desires he is bound to offer to Me for his neighbor. Every act of help he performs should proceed from the compassion he has because of his love for Me."

Teach me Your love today.

FEBRUARY 3

If I give away all my possessions, and if I hand over my body so that I may boast, but do not have love, I gain nothing.
—1 Corinthians 13:3 (NRSV)

"Do you remember our Lord's words on these subjects? To the rich man, Jesus says, 'If you wish to be perfect, go, sell your possessions, and give the money to the poor, and you will have treasure in heaven; then come, follow me' (Matt. 19:21). And when he is teaching about love to one's neighbor, Jesus also says, 'No one has greater love than this, to lay down one's life for one's friends' (John 15:13). From teachings such as these, it is evident

that even before God, love is the greatest commandment of all."
—St. John Chrysostom

> **Sometimes I think that I don't even know
> what love means, God. Show me.**

=== **FEBRUARY 4** ===

𝒜s a body is one though it has many parts, and all the parts
of the body, though many, are one body, so also Christ.
—1 Corinthians 12:12 (NAB)

"Love for each other is of very great importance. Anything, no matter how annoying, can be easily borne by those who love each other. Anything that causes annoyance must be quite exceptional. If the world kept this commandment, I believe it would take us a long way toward keeping the rest."
—St. Teresa of Avila

> **What may I do to build up the body of Christ?**

=== **FEBRUARY 5** ===

ℒet my cry come before you, O LORD; give me
understanding according to your word.
—Psalm 119:169 (NRSV)

"[St. Antony] very often spent the entire night in prayer and ate only once a day, after sunset. Sometimes he continued fasting for two or three days at a time and only ate and drank on the fourth day. He ate bread and salt, and drank a little water. I think it is better not to say anything about his consumption of meat and wine, for most monks do not consume either one. When he did allow himself to rest, he used a woven rush mat covered with goat's hair. Sometimes he would simply lie on the bare ground, and he refused to anoint his body with oil. For he used to say that it is hardly possible that the bodies of those who use such things, and especially young men's bodies, should grow strong if they are softened by smooth oil. Instead they ought to use rigorous exercises to control the flesh, as the apostle Paul said: 'Therefore I am content with weaknesses, insults, hardships, persecutions, and calamities for the sake of Christ; for whenever I am weak, then I am strong' (2 Cor. 12:10)." —St. Athanasius

O God, You know I'm no saint! But, today, make me just a little more like one.

= FEBRUARY 6 =

*M*y lips will pour forth praise, because
you teach me your statutes.
—Psalm 119:171 (NRSV)

"Someone asked Antony, 'What must one do in order to please God?' He replied, 'Pay attention to what I tell you. Whoever you may be, always have God before your eyes. Whatever you do, do it according to the testimony of the Holy Scriptures. Wherever you live, do not easily leave it. Keep these three precepts and you will be saved." —*The Wisdom of the Desert Fathers and Mothers*

I will practice these three things: keeping God before my eyes, reading the Holy Scriptures, and being steadfast.

=== FEBRUARY 7 ===

And we know that for those who love God all things
work together for good, for those who are called
according to his purpose.
—Romans 8:28 (ESV)

"God gave me the grace to open my intelligence quite early and to engrave so deeply in my memory the remembrances of my childhood that it seems to me that the things that I'm going to tell about happened yesterday. Without a doubt, Jesus wanted, in His love, to make me know the incomparable mother that He gave me, but whom His Divine hand was hastening to crown in Heaven!" —St. Thérèse of Lisieux

Many of us have been blessed with parents who taught us to love God. Let us give thanks.

*F*or surely I know the plans I have for you, says the Lord, plans for your welfare and not for harm, to give you a future with hope. —Jeremiah 29:11 (nrsv)

"Everything on earth and in heaven compared with God is nothing, as Jeremiah says in these words: 'I beheld the earth, and it was empty, and it was nothing; I beheld the heavens, and saw that they had no light. When he looked at the heavens and saw no light in them, he says that all the bright stars in the skies, compared with God, are pure darkness. All created things are nothing and their passions are less than nothing, since they are impediments to transformation in God. The soul that expends its passions on created things will not be able to comprehend God, for until it is cleansed it will not be able to possess God, either on this earth through pure transformation of love, or beyond this earth with a clear vision.'" —St. John of the Cross

My soul rests, and waits, in You.

*F*or this is the message you have heard from the beginning, that we should love one another. —1 John 3:11 (nrsv)

Christ spoke thus to St. Catherine of Siena: "Love of Me and of one's neighbor are one and the same thing; and, so far as the soul loves Me, it loves its neighbor, because love toward one's neighbor issues from Me. This is the means I have given you, so that you may exercise and prove your virtue; because, inasmuch as you can do Me no profit, you should do good to your neighbor. This proves that you possess Me by grace in your soul, producing much fruit for your neighbor and making prayers to Me, as you seek with sweet and loving desire My honor and the salvation of souls.'"

Show me my "neighbor" today, Lord. I promise I will respond.

FEBRUARY 10

$\mathcal{I}$ kneel before the Father, from whom every family in heaven and on earth is named, that he may grant you in accord with the riches of his glory to be strengthened with power through his Spirit in the inner self, and that Christ may dwell in your hearts through faith. —Ephesians 3:14–17a (NAB)

"The mystic who passes through the moment when there is nothing but God does in some sense behold the beginningless beginnings in which there was really nothing else. He not only appreciates everything but the nothing of which everything was made. In a fashion he endures and answers even the earthquake irony of the Book of Job; in some sense he is there when the foundations of the world are laid, with the morning stars singing together and the sons of God shouting for joy."

—G. K. Chesterton, writing about St. Francis of Assisi

I praise You, Lord God, for the grandeur of Your Creation. Please show it to me in fresh ways today.

[There is only] one body and one Spirit, as you were
also called to the one hope of your call; one Lord,
one faith, one baptism; one God and Father of all,
who is over all and through all and in all.
—Ephesians 4:4–6 (NAB)

"It may seem that to have too much love for each other cannot be wrong, but I do not think anyone who had not witnessed it would believe how much evil and how many imperfections can result from this. The consciences of those who aim at pleasing God in provisional ways seldom observe the devil's snares. They think they are acting virtuously. . . . For example, a nun desires to have something to give to her friend or tries to make time for talking to her. Often her object is to tell her how fond she is of her, and other irrelevant things, rather than how much she loves God. But these intimate friendships rarely focus on the love of God. . . . In our community, we must all be friends with each other, love each other, be fond of each other, and help each other." —St. Teresa of Avila

**Thank You for those who love me. But I know that
You are my first and truest love.**

FEBRUARY 12

Therefore I am content with weaknesses, insults, hardships, persecutions, and calamities for the sake of Christ; for whenever I am weak, then I am strong.
—2 Corinthians 12:10 (NRSV)

"How good God is! How He apportions out trials according to the strength that He gives us." —St. Thérèse of Lisieux

Whatever I struggle with today, Lord, is what You know I can handle. Thank You for that.

FEBRUARY 13

[*Jesus* said,] "Watch and pray so that you will not fall into temptation. The spirit is willing, but the flesh is weak."
—Matthew 26:41 (NIV)

"Father Antony said, 'This is the great work of a person: always to take the blame for his or her own sins before God and to expect temptation until the last breath.' He also said, 'Whoever has not experienced temptation cannot enter into the kingdom of heaven.' He even added, 'Without temptation no one can be saved.'" —*The Wisdom of the Desert Fathers and Mothers*

Holy Spirit, I may be desensitized to temptation. Don't let me sleepwalk through this day. Make me more vigilant in serving You.

FEBRUARY 14

After they prayed, the place where they were meeting was
shaken. And they were all filled with the Holy Spirit and
spoke the word of God boldly.
—Acts 4:31 (NIV)

"Sr. Elena is eighty-seven years old, blind, and spends her days
in a wheelchair. I didn't notice her when I began preaching the
weeklong retreat at the retirement home where she resides. But
on the afternoon of the second day, she asked someone to push
her to me. 'Father, I have a secret to tell you,' she said. I leaned
over and she whispered in my ear, 'God l-o-n-g-s to turn you
into a saint!' Her face lit up as she added, 'If you respond to God's
yearning, you'll be amazed at what happens.'"
—Fr. Albert Haase, OFM

I am responding now, Lord. What do You want me to do?

FEBRUARY 15

"*The* Surface of Things"
by Br. Paul Quenon, OCSO

Is everything really illusion?
Might I pass through this heavy oak door
without opening it?

I lean gently to and feel it yield to weight,
swaying in agreement—
my respect for its solidity,
to my passage it yields a breath of concession.

Jesus had such exquisite care
not to disturb the surface of water
that He could walk on it.

Oh God, I want to know You, beyond what I can see.

═══ FEBRUARY 16 ═══

There are different kinds of gifts, but the same Spirit
distributes them. There are different kinds of service, but
the same Lord. There are different kinds of working, but in
all of them and in everyone it is the same God at work.
—1 Corinthians 12:4–6 (NIV)

Christ explained to St. Catherine of Siena: "In many cases I give
one virtue to be the chief of the others. That is to say, to one
person I will give principally love, to another principally justice,
to another principally humility, or a lively faith, or prudence, or
temperance, or patience, or fortitude. I could easily have created
people possessed of all that they should need both for body and
soul, but I desire that one should have need of the other, and that
they should be My ministers to administer the graces and the
gifts they have received from Me."

Holy Father, show me who needs me, and who I need, today.

FEBRUARY 17

$\mathcal{T}$o all those in Rome who are loved by God and
called to be saints: Grace to you and peace from
God our Father and the Lord Jesus Christ.
—Romans 1:7 (ESV)

"[An] attraction to reading lasted until my entrance into Carmel.
It would be impossible for me to say how many books passed
through my hands, but God never allowed me to read a single
one that was capable of harming me. It's true that as I read certain tales about knights, I didn't always feel at first glance the
truth about life; but soon God let me feel that true glory is the
one that will last forever, and that to obtain it, it isn't necessary
to do outstanding works, but to remain hidden and to practice
virtue. So, when I was reading the tales of the patriotic actions
of French heroines, in particular those of the Venerable Joan of
Arc, I had a great desire to imitate them. It seemed to me that
I felt within me the same burning desire that stirred them, the
same heavenly inspiration." —St. Thérèse of Lisieux

Inspire me, Lord, to serve You with boldness.

FEBRUARY 18

$\mathcal{S}$ee what love the Father has given us, that we should be
called children of God; and that is what we are. The reason the
world does not know us is that it did not know him.
—1 John 3:1 (NRSV)

"It seems to me that one loves very differently from others when one has learned the great difference between this world and the other one. This world is only a dream and the other is eternal. One who knows the difference between loving the Creator and loving the creature also knows the difference between purely spiritual love and spiritual love mingled with sensuality. Those who have devoted themselves to being taught by God in prayer also love very differently from those who lack such devotion."
—St. Teresa of Avila

I want to love You; sometimes I don't know how.

FEBRUARY 19

*P*lace these words on your hearts. Get them deep inside you. Tie them on your hands and foreheads as a reminder. Teach them to your children. Talk about them wherever you are, sitting at home or walking in the street; talk about them from the time you get up in the morning until you fall into bed at night. Inscribe them on the doorposts and gates of your cities so that you'll live a long time, and your children with you, on the soil that GOD promised to give your ancestors for as long as there is a sky over the Earth.
—Deuteronomy 11:18–21 (THE MESSAGE)

"One day, when the brothers who had gathered there were asking the holy Antony to provide some guidelines for their way of life, he raised his voice with a prophet's confidence and said that the Scriptures were sufficient for all teaching of the rule. He taught also that it would be an excellent idea for the brothers to support each other with mutual encouragement." —St. Athanasius

**I am reminded, Lord, that Your Holy Scriptures
contain all the wisdom I require.**

═══ FEBRUARY 20 ═══

*T*hose who guard their mouths and their tongues
keep themselves from calamity.
—Proverbs 21:23 (NIV)

"Father Pambo asked Father Antony, 'What ought I to do?' Antony replied, 'Do not trust in your own righteousness, do not worry about the past, but control your tongue and your stomach.'" —*The Wisdom of the Desert Fathers and Mothers*

**Gossip and indulgence, Father—save me from both today.
Please remind me when to shut my mouth.**

═══ FEBRUARY 21 ═══

O God, come to my assistance; O Lord, make haste to help me.
—Psalm 70:1 (DOUAY-RHEIMS)

"Like many Catholics, I grew up in a family that recited the rosary every night. And we knew why we did; as Mom would often assure us, the most effective person to take our prayers to Jesus was His own mother. As a good son, how could He refuse her?

"As children, we often came to the nightly rosary with protest—'in a minute, Ma'—but having settled on our knees, it was a lovely, quieting time, one that bonded our family of nine kids at the end of a day of the usual sibling tensions. Years later, when we gathered for our parents' wakes, and then for those of siblings, we prayed the rosary together and it bonded us still. The rosary crusader Father Paddy Peyton was right when he said, 'The family that prays together, stays together.'" —Thomas Groome

Our Father. . . .
Hail Mary. . . .
Glory be. . . .

FEBRUARY 22

Take delight in the LORD, and he will give
you the desires of your heart.
—Psalm 37:4 (NIV)

"The delights and pleasures of the will in the things of the world, in comparison with God's delights, are supreme affliction, torment, and bitterness. One who sets his heart on them is considered in God's sight as worthy of supreme affliction, torment, and bitterness. He will be unable to gain the delights of embracing union with God. . . . The soul that loves and possesses creature wealth is supremely poor and wretched in God's sight, and for that reason will be unable to gain the wealth and glory that is the state of transformation in God." —St. John of the Cross

Am I being transformed in You, Lord? How will I know?

══ FEBRUARY 23 ══

If I give everything I own to the poor and even go to the
stake to be burned as a martyr, but I don't love, I've gotten
nowhere. So, no matter what I say, what I believe,
and what I do, I'm bankrupt without love.
—1 Corinthians 13:3 (THE MESSAGE)

St. Catherine of Siena heard Christ say to her: "I wish for no other thing than love. For in the love of Me is fulfilled and completed the love of one's neighbor, and the law is observed. For only those who are bound to Me with this love can be of use in their state of life."

Father, show me a new way to love one of my friends, today.

══ FEBRUARY 24 ══

Now the people of Judah approached Joshua at Gilgal,
and Caleb son of Jephunneh the Kenizzite said to him, "You
know what the LORD said to Moses the man of God at Kadesh
Barnea about you and me. I was forty years old when Moses

the servant of the LORD sent me from Kadesh Barnea to explore the land. And I brought him back a report according to my convictions, but my fellow Israelites who went up with me made the hearts of the people melt in fear. I, however, followed the LORD my God wholeheartedly. So on that day Moses swore to me, 'The land on which your feet have walked will be your inheritance and that of your children forever, because you have followed the LORD my God wholeheartedly.'"
—Joshua 14:6–9 (NIV)

"Catching and crackling with the fire of godly enthusiasm is a lifelong process. It starts with God throwing a divine spark on the tinder of the heart. . . . It might be an attraction or religious sentiment that grips the heart. It might be an event or situation that stirs your devotion. It could even be a word spoken by a friend, colleague, or relative which gets underneath the skin and stings your conscience." —Fr. Albert Haase, OFM

What is keeping me from wholeheartedly following You?

FEBRUARY 25

"But the Helper, the Holy Spirit, whom the Father will send in my name, he will teach you all things and bring to your remembrance all that I have said to you."
—John 14:26 (ESV)

"One day one of my teachers at the Abbey school asked me what I did on my days off when I was alone. I replied that I would go behind my bed into an empty space that was there and that was easy for me to shut off with the curtain, and there, 'I would think.' 'But what do you think about?' she said. 'I think about God, about life . . . about ETERNITY, I just think!' The good nun laughed a lot at me. Later she liked to remind me of the time when I used to think, and asked me if I was still thinking. I understand now that I was praying at length without knowing it, and that already God was teaching me in secret." —St. Thérèse of Lisieux

Please teach me in secret today, Lord.

═══ FEBRUARY 26 ═══

[O]n all your ways submit to him, and he will
make your paths straight.
—Proverbs 3:6 (NIV)

"When we desire anyone's affection we always seek it because of some interest, profit, or pleasure of our own. Those who are perfect, though, have trampled all these things beneath their feet. They have so despised this world's pleasures, delights, and blessings that they could not love anything outside God or unless it has to do with God. What can they gain, then, from being loved themselves?" —St. Teresa of Avila

I want only You.

FEBRUARY 27

I have been crucified with Christ and I no
longer live, but Christ lives in me.
—Galatians 2:20a (NIV)

"Antony said, 'Just as fish die if they stay too long out of water,
so the monks who loiter outside their prayer chambers or pass
their time with men of the world lose the intensity of their inner
peace. So, like a fish going toward the sea, we must hurry to reach
our prayer chamber. If we delay outside, we will lose our interior
watchfulness.'" —*The Wisdom of the Desert Fathers and Mothers*

**I am a fish today, God, wanting to spend
time in Your cool, dark waters.**

FEBRUARY 28

*M*ary said, "Behold, I am the handmaid of the Lord.
May it be done to me according to your word."
—Luke 1:38 (NAB)

"If, as St. Augustine thought, prayer is our saying things together
with Christ and His saying them with us, it follows that there
can be no greater teacher of prayer, after Christ Himself, than
His mother, Mary. 'After Christ' in hierarchical order, not in the
temporal, because in the order of time it was obviously Mary
who taught little Jesus 'his prayers,' as all believing mothers do
with their children as soon as they can pronounce the words,

even badly. We should imagine the Virgin saying a prayer with her son, and He then saying it with her. [I]n His supreme hour at Gethsemane Jesus . . . reproduce[d] Mary's original 'Fiat.' . . . [I]n human terms and in the order of time, the Son of God learned other prayers too, and His style of prayer with its attitudes and gestures, from His mother." —Timothy Verdon

Teach me, Mother of God, to pray.

═ FEBRUARY 29 ═

"Monk's Prayer"
by Bonnie Thurston

At the monastic center
is always a cloister,
an orchestrated emptiness,
a place of light,
a fountain to feed
the heart's garden.

Give me this life:
a center empty
of all but light,
the stillness of Eden
before fruit was plucked,
my heart a spring
of living water.

My heart is a cloister for only You, today.

March

═══ MARCH 1 ═══

"Whoever wants to be great must become a servant. Whoever wants to be first among you must be your slave. That is what the Son of Man has done: He came to serve, not to be served."
—Mark 10:44–45a (The Message)

St. Catherine of Siena heard Christ say to her, "A person proves his patience by means of his neighbor when he receives injuries from him. Similarly, he proves his humility through a proud man, his faith through a faithless one, his true hope through one who despairs, his justice through the unjust, his kindness through the cruel, and his gentleness and graciousness through the irascible. Good people produce and prove all their virtues through their neighbor, just as perverse people do all their vices."

Teach me kindness, graciousness, and humility today.

═══ MARCH 2 ═══

Does not the dew give relief from the scorching heat?
So a word is better than a gift.
Indeed, does not a word surpass a good gift?
Both are to be found in a gracious person.
—Sirach 18:16–17 (NRSV)

"Christ Himself says, 'I desire mercy and not sacrifice,' echoing Hos. 6:6, 'For I desire steadfast love and not sacrifice, the knowledge of God rather than burnt offerings.' Because it is common

for us to love those who benefited from us, and for those who receive benefits to be kinder toward their benefactors, Jesus made this law, constituting it as a bond of friendship."
—St. John Chrysostom

I will try and love someone, today, whom I find difficult to love.

=== MARCH 3 ===

May the eyes of (your) hearts be enlightened, that you may know what is the hope that belongs to [the Father of glory's] call, what are the riches of glory in his inheritance. . . .
—Ephesians 1:18 (NAB)

"That we all depend in every detail, at every instant, as a Christian would say upon God, as even an agnostic would say upon existence and the nature of things, is not an illusion of imagination; on the contrary, it is the fundamental fact which we cover up, as with curtains, with the illusion of ordinary life."
—G. K. Chesterton

**Father, my own understanding is worthless—
without Your illumination.**

=== MARCH 4 ===

Little children, you are from God and have overcome them, for he who is in you is greater than he who is in the world.
—1 John 4:4 (ESV)

"Those into whose souls the Lord has already infused true wisdom do not value this love, which lasts only on earth, for more than it is worth. Those who take pleasure in worldly things, delights, honors, and riches will judge it of some value if their friend is rich and can afford to bring them worldly pleasures. Those who already hate all this will care little or nothing for such things. If they have any love for such a person, it will be a passion that he may love God so as to be loved by God. They know that no other kind of affection can last and that this kind will cost them dearly. For this reason they do all they possibly can for the good of their friend. They would lose a thousand lives to bring him a small blessing. Oh precious love . . . !" —St. Teresa of Avila

Give me the courage today, Father, to represent You.

═══ MARCH 5 ═══

*B*lessed be the God and Father of our Lord Jesus Christ,
who has blessed us in Christ with every spiritual blessing in
the heavens, as he chose us in him, before the foundation
of the world, to be holy and without blemish before him.
—Ephesians 1:3–4 (NAB)

"The brothers praised a monk before Antony. When the monk came to see him, Antony wanted to know how he would bear insults. Seeing that he could not bear them at all, Antony said to him, 'You are like a village magnificently decorated on the outside, but destroyed from within by robbers.' Someone else said to Antony, 'Pray for me.' The old man said to him, 'I will have no mercy upon you, nor will God have any, if you yourself do not make an effort, and if you do not pray to God.'"

—*The Wisdom of the Desert Fathers and Mothers*

Search me, God, and find what is false in me. I trust You.

=== **MARCH 6** ===

*J*esus answered them, "In this godless world you will
continue to experience difficulties. But take heart!
I've conquered the world."
—John 16:33 (THE MESSAGE)

"Don't let yourselves grow weary. Do not be seduced by pride in your achievement. For 'the sufferings of this present time are not worth comparing with the glory about to be revealed to us' (Rom. 8:18). No one, once he has rejected this world, should think he has left behind anything important. The entire earth, compared to the infinity of the heavens, is small and limited. Even if we renounce the whole world, we cannot give anything in exchange that is of similar value to the heavenly dwellings. If each person considers this, he will immediately realize that if he abandons a few acres of land or a small house or a moderate sum of gold, he ought not to feel proud of himself in the belief that he has given up a lot." —St. Antony, as told by St. Athanasius

Remind me all day, today, Lord, of what is most important.

$\mathcal{G}$od rained manna upon them for food; grain from
heaven he gave them. Man ate the bread of the
angels; food he sent in abundance.
—Psalm 78:24–25 (NAB)

"If spiritual people only knew how much good they lose and what great fullness of spirit they lose when they do not raise their desires above childish things. If only they did not have the desire to taste worldly things, they would find the sweetness of all things in this simple spiritual food. But spiritual food gives them no pleasure for the same reason that the children of Israel did not taste the sweetness of all foods that the manna contained; they did not set apart their desire for it alone. They failed to find in the manna all the sweetness and strength that they could want, not because the manna did not contain these things, but because they desired something else. People who love some other thing together with God make little account of Him."
—St. John of the Cross

Show me how to love You, Lord.

$\mathcal{T}$hose who say, "I love God," and hate their brothers or sisters,
are liars; for those who do not love a brother or sister whom
they have seen, cannot love God whom they have not seen.
—1 John 4:20 (NRSV)

Christ spoke to St. Catherine of Siena: "These are the fruits and the works that I seek from the soul, namely, the proving of virtue in the time of need. And yet some time ago, when you wanted to do great penance for My sake, and asked, 'What can I do to endure suffering for You, Lord?' I replied to you, 'I take delight in few words and many works.'"

I want to serve You. Show me what I can do today, Holy Spirit.

MARCH 9

"For where thy treasure is, there is thy heart also."
—Matthew 6:21 (DOUAY-RHEIMS)

In her spiritual memoir, *The Story of a Soul*, St. Thérèse of Lisieux writes, "I don't want to enter into the details. Just as there are things that lose their sweet scent as soon as they are exposed to the air, there are also thoughts of the soul that cannot be interpreted in the language of the earth without losing their intimate and heavenly feeling. They are like that white stone that will be given to those who are victorious and on which is written a new name that no one knows other than the one who receives it [cf. Rev. 2:17]."

Thank You, God. Thank You. Now, I'll be quiet.

MARCH 10

$\mathscr{P}$ursue love, and earnestly desire the spiritual gifts.
—1 Corinthians 14:1a (ESV)

"The mere awareness of being attracted to prayer or wanting to make God some part of daily life is the beginning of the process of being transformed. Before that awareness, we are like sleepwalkers. Life is a task-oriented game characterized by a flatness, sluggishness, and sometimes lackluster monotony. Many are quite content to live this way. . . . Sooner or later we all discover that restlessness comes into our lives for a profound purpose—in order for us to begin a relationship with God. This is the awakening." —Fr. Albert Haase, OFM

**If I am feeling spiritually restless, I will pause to pray.
I will ask God to reveal to me why.**

MARCH 11

$\mathscr{J}$esus said: "I am the good shepherd. A good
shepherd lays down his life for the sheep."
—John 10:11 (NAB)

"It is strange to see how much passion this love provokes. It costs many tears, penances, and prayers. The loving soul is careful to commend the object of its affection to all who it thinks may prevail with God and to ask them to intercede with him for this object of affection. The loving soul's longing is constant, and it cannot be happy unless it sees that its loved one is making progress. If the latter seems to have advanced and then falls back, her friend seems to have no pleasure in life. She does not eat or sleep and is always afraid that the soul whom she loves so much may be lost, and that the two may be parted forever. She is not concerned about physical death, but she cannot bear to be attached to something that a puff of wind may suddenly carry away. This is love without any degree of self-interest. All that this soul wishes is to see the soul it loves enriched with blessings from heaven. This is love that grows to be more like Christ's love for us. It deserves the name of love and is quite different from our petty and frivolous earthly affections." —St. Teresa of Avila

I know that You loved me long before I loved You.

══ MARCH 12 ══

$\mathcal{G}$reat are your judgments and hard to describe.
—Wisdom 17:1a (NRSV)

"One day some old men came to see Antony. Father Joseph was in their midst. Wanting to test them, the old man suggested a text from the Scriptures, and, beginning with the youngest, he asked them what it meant. Each gave his opinion, as he was able. But to each one the old man said, 'You have not understood it.' Finally he said to Joseph, 'How would you explain this saying?'

Joseph said, 'I do not know.' Then Antony said, 'Indeed, Joseph has found the way, for he has said, "I do not know."'"
—*The Wisdom of the Desert Fathers and Mothers*

Bless me in my doubts, today, Lord.

═══ MARCH 13 ═══

*C*onsider this: . . . whoever sows bountifully
will also reap bountifully.
—2 Corinthians 9:6 (NAB)

"In order to arrive at having pleasure in everything,
Desire to have pleasure in nothing.
In order to arrive at possessing everything,
Desire to possess nothing."
—St. John of the Cross [continued tomorrow . . .]

I don't really want anything but You.

═══ MARCH 14 ═══

*L*ORD, you have probed me, you know me: you know when I
sit and stand; you understand my thoughts from afar.
—Psalm 139:1–2 (NAB)

"In order to arrive at being everything,
Desire to be nothing.

In order to arrive at knowing everything,
Desire to know nothing."
—St. John of the Cross [continued tomorrow . . .]

I am content not knowing.

═══ MARCH 15 ═══

*Y*ou sift through my travels and my rest; with all my
ways you are familiar. Even before a word is
on my tongue, LORD, you know it all.
—Psalm 139:3–4 (NAB)

"In order to arrive at the place where you have no pleasure,
You must go by a way in which you have no pleasure.
In order to arrive at what you do not know,
You must go by a way that you do not know."
—St. John of the Cross [continued tomorrow . . .]

There is comfort in knowing that I don't always have to know.

═══ MARCH 16 ═══

*I*f I take the wings of dawn and dwell beyond the sea, even
there your hand guides me, your right hand holds me fast.
—Psalm 139:9–10 (NAB)

"In order to arrive at what you do not possess,
You must go by a way that you do not possess.
In order to arrive at what you are not,
You must go through what you are not."
—St. John of the Cross [continued tomorrow . . .]

Only You know the real me.

𝒫robe me, God, know my heart; try me, know my thoughts.
—Psalm 139:23 (NAB)

"When your mind dwells on anything,
You are ceasing to cast yourself on the All.
For, in order to pass from the all to the All,
You have to deny yourself wholly in all."
—St. John of the Cross [continued tomorrow . . .]

I am me only in light of You.

𝓛ove GOD, your God, with your whole heart: love him
with all that's in you, love him with all you've got!
—Deuteronomy 6:5 (THE MESSAGE)

"And when you come to possess [the All] wholly,
You must possess it without desiring anything.
For if you will have anything in having all,
You do not have your treasure purely in God."
—St. John of the Cross

May the love I feel today become the love I show.

═══ MARCH 19 ═══

$\mathcal{F}$or as Christ's sufferings overflow to us, so through
Christ does our encouragement also overflow.
—2 Corinthians 1:5 (NAB)

As Christ spoke to St. Catherine of Siena: "Just as one more readily sees spots on one's face by looking in a mirror, so the soul that, with true knowledge of self, rises with desire and gazes with the eye of the intellect at itself in the sweet mirror of God, knows better the stains of its own face by the purity it sees in Him."

I praise You, Lord. Like an angel at Your feet, I praise You.

═══ MARCH 20 ═══

"$\mathcal{T}$hou shalt love the Lord thy God with thy whole heart,
and with thy whole soul, and with all thy strength, and
with all thy mind: and thy neighbor as thyself."
—Luke 10:27 (DOUAY-RHEIMS)

"Some brothers came to Antony and said to him, 'Tell us: How are we to be saved?' The old man said to them, 'You have heard the Scriptures. That should teach you how.' But they said, 'We want to hear from you, too, father.' Then the old man said to them, 'The Gospel says: if anyone strikes you on the right cheek, turn the other also.' They said, 'We cannot do that.' The old man said, 'If you cannot offer the other cheek, at least allow one cheek to be struck.' 'We cannot do that, either,' they said. So he said, 'If you are not able to do that, do not return evil for evil,' and they said, 'We cannot do that, either.' Then the old man said to his disciples, 'If you cannot do this, or that, what can I do for you? What you need is prayers.'"

—*The Wisdom of the Desert Fathers and Mothers*

I know what I need to do, Father. Now, give me courage.

═ MARCH 21 ═

To you, O LORD, I lift up my soul, my God, in you I trust.
—Psalm 25:1–2a (NAB)

"Someone asked Father Moses, 'What good is fasting?' The old man said, 'It makes the soul humble. For it is written, "Consider my affliction and my trouble, and forgive all my sins" (Ps. 25:18). So if the soul gives itself all this hardship, God will have mercy on it.'" —*The Wisdom of the Desert Fathers and Mothers*

**I will fast today, and the hunger I feel will
remind of my hunger for You.**

MARCH 22

$\mathcal{T}$he LORD is my light and my salvation; whom do I fear? —
Psalm 27:1a (NAB)

"Before ascending the mount, any soul that wants to ascend the mount to offer God the sacrifice of pure love and praise must do three things. First, it must cast away all foreign gods—that is, all passions and attachments foreign to God. Second, through the dark night of the senses it must purify itself of the remnants that the desires have left in the soul, by habitually denying them and relieving itself of them. Third, in order to reach this high mountaintop, it must have changed its garments."
—St. John of the Cross

Show me today what I haven't yet cast away for You.

MARCH 23

$\mathcal{H}$ow sweet are your words to my taste,
sweeter than honey to my mouth!
—Psalm 119:103 (NIV)

"Often during my Communions, I would repeat these words from the *Imitation of Christ*: 'O Jesus, inexpressible sweetness, change for me into bitterness, all the consolations of the earth.' This prayer came out of my lips without effort, without constraint. It seemed to me that I was repeating it, not by my will, but like a child who repeats the words that a friend inspires in her. Later I will tell you, beloved Mother, how Jesus was pleased to make my desire come true, how He was always, He alone, my inexpressible sweetness." —St. Thérèse of Lisieux

You are sweet, Lord. I will remember Your sweetness throughout this day.

MARCH 24

But shun profane and vain babblings: for
they grow much towards ungodliness.
—2 Timothy 2:16 (DOUAY-RHEIMS)

"We do not need ever to take frivolous affections to our lips, or even think of them, or to remember that they exist anywhere in the world. Do not ever listen to anyone speaking of such things, either seriously or humorously, and do not allow them to be mentioned or discussed in your presence. No good can come from our discussing them." —St. Teresa of Avila

Holy Spirit, give me courage. Guard my mind. Strengthen my spirit with Your truth.

$\mathcal{T}$oday is the Feast of the Annunciation
to the Blessed Virgin Mary

"Mary receives the Spirit, thus transforming an historical event into a spiritual happening. . . . St. Augustine says: 'Mary was happy for this very reason: she heard God's word and kept it. In fact she kept the truth in her mind even more than the flesh in her womb. Christ is truth, Christ is flesh, Christ is the truth in Mary's mind and the flesh in her womb. But what she bore in her mind counts for more than what she bore in her womb.' In the same vein St. Leo the Great would later say that Mary 'conceived the Son, the Man-God, first in her heart and then in her body.'"
—Timothy Verdon

**I will say "yes" to You today, with my life,
just as our Mother Mary did so readily.**

══ **MARCH 26** ══

$\mathcal{T}$he sound of my lover! Here he comes springing
across the mountains, leaping across the hills.
—Song of Songs 2:8 (NAB)

"Oh, abyss of love! What heart can help breaking when it sees such dignity as Yours descend to such lowliness as our humanity? We are Your image, and You have become ours, by this union that You have accomplished with man, veiling the eternal Deity with the cloud of woe and the corrupted clay of Adam. For what reason?—Love." —St. Catherine of Siena

Thank You for loving me!

═ MARCH 27 ═

*H*e rescued us from such great danger of death,
and he will continue to rescue us; in him we have
put our hope [that] he will also rescue us again.
—2 Corinthians 1:10 (NAB)

"One day a monk in another monastery was tempted. Cast out of the monastery, he went over the mountain to Antony. The brother lived near him for a while, and then Antony sent him back to the monastery from which he had been expelled. When the brothers saw him, they cast him out again. He returned to Antony, saying, 'My Father, they will not receive me.' Then the old man sent them a message saying, 'A boat was shipwrecked at sea and lost its cargo. It reached the shore with great difficulty. You want to throw into the sea that which has found a safe harbor on the shore.' When the brothers understood that it was Antony who had sent them this monk, they received him at once."
—*The Wisdom of the Desert Fathers and Mothers*

I sometimes feel like a shipwreck, God.
Help me find my way to shore.

MARCH 28

$\mathcal{G}$ive thanks to the LORD, for he is good,
his mercy endures forever.
—Psalm 118:1 (NAB)

"The whole point about St. Francis of Assisi is that he certainly was ascetical and he certainly was not gloomy. As soon as ever he had been unhorsed by the glorious humiliation of his vision of dependence on the divine love, he flung himself into fasting and vigil exactly as he had flung himself furiously into battle. . . . There was nothing negative about it; it was not a regimen or a stoical simplicity of life. It was not self-denial merely in the sense of self-control. It was as positive as a passion; it had all the air of being as positive as a pleasure. He devoured fasting as a man devours food." —G. K. Chesterton

Give me renewed vigor for fasting, so I can focus on You.

MARCH 29

$\mathcal{T}$hen Jesus told them a parable about their need
to pray always and not to lose heart.
—Luke 18:1 (NRSV)

"The agony in the garden with which Christ's passion began [is] considered emblematic of perfect prayer [and] illustrate[s] the Savior's teaching that it is necessary to pray always. . . . It genuinely reassumes every other prayer that human beings can imagine, and in its light Christ, constituted head of the body of a new humanity, becomes, in St. Augustine's words, 'the one who prays for us, the one who prays in us, the one to whom we pray. He prays for us as our priest; He prays in us as our head; we pray to Him as our God.'" —Timothy Verdon

**I know that I can pray everything to You.
You want all of me, good and bad.**

═══ MARCH 30 ═══

*J*esus said to them again, "Peace be with you. As the Father has sent me, so I send you." When he had said this, he breathed on them and said to them, "Receive the Holy Spirit. If you forgive the sins of any, they are forgiven them; if you retain the sins of any, they are retained."
—John 20:21–23 (NRSV)

"Well instructed in what I should say and do, I went into the confessional and knelt down, but when he opened the grille Father Ducellier didn't see anyone. I was so little that my head was below the little shelf on which people fold their hands. So he told me to stand up. Obeying immediately, I stood up and, turning directly toward him so I could see him well, I made my confession . . . and I received his blessing with great devotion, because you had told me that at that moment the tears of the Baby Jesus were going to purify my soul. I remember that the first exhortation that was addressed to me invited me especially to devotion to the Blessed Virgin, and I promised to redouble my tenderness toward her. When I left the confessional I was so happy and so light that I've never felt so much joy in my soul. Afterward I returned to confess at every important holiday, and it was a true celebration for me each time I went." —St. Thérèse of Lisieux

Give me the faith of a child, God.

═══ MARCH 31 ═══

[C]omplete my joy by being of the same mind,
with the same love, united in heart. . . .
—Philippians 2:2 (NAB)

"I repeat that [true, spiritual affection] is just like the love that Jesus, the good Lover, bore for us. It brings us such immense benefits, for it makes us embrace every kind of suffering, so that others, without having to endure the suffering, may gain its advantage. The recipients of such friendship gain much. . . . Their heart does not allow them to be false. If they see their friend straying from the road, they will speak to her about it. They cannot allow themselves to do anything else." —St. Teresa of Avila

**Show me how to be true to my brothers
and sisters in Christ, today.**

April

"*O*nly fear the Lord and serve him faithfully with all your heart. For consider what great things he has done for you."
—1 Samuel 12:24 (ESV)

"Let us bear in mind that we are servants of the Lord and that we owe a service to Him who created us. For a servant does not reject present or future authority on account of past service, and does not dare to claim that because of his past he ought to be released from the task at hand. Instead, he continues to perform the same service with unbroken commitment so as to please his master and so that his wages will not be fear and beatings. In the same way it is right for us to obey the divine commandments, knowing that he who is a just judge will judge each person where He finds him." —St. Antony, as told by St. Athanasius

What is my service to God?

*S*ee to it that no one captivate you with an empty, seductive philosophy according to human tradition, according to the elemental powers of the world and not according to Christ.
—Colossians 2:8 (NAB)

"Father Ammonas once said, 'A person can spend his whole time carrying an axe without succeeding in cutting down the tree. Another person, who has experience in chopping down trees, brings the tree down with a few blows. He said that the axe is discernment." —*The Wisdom of the Desert Fathers and Mothers*

Holy Spirit, teach me greater discernment today.

═══ APRIL 3 ═══

*A*sk rain from the LORD in the season of the spring rain,
from the LORD who makes the storm clouds, who gives
showers of rain to you, the vegetation in the field to everyone.
—Zechariah 10:1 (NRSV)

St. Catherine heard these words of God: "The truth is that I have created humanity in My own image and likeness, so that they might have eternal life, and might partake of Me and taste My supreme and eternal sweetness and goodness. But after sin had closed heaven and bolted the doors of mercy, the soul of man produced thorns and prickly brambles, and My creature found in himself rebellion against himself."

I want to find my likeness in You, today.

═══ APRIL 4 ═══

*F*or God did not send his Son into the world to condemn the
world, but that the world might be saved through him.
—John 3:17 (NAB)

As God spoke to St. Catherine of Siena: "As soon as humanity had sinned, there arose a tempestuous flood, which continues to buffet them with its waves, bringing them weariness and trouble from themselves, the devil, and the world. Everyone was drowned in the flood, because no one, with his own righteousness alone, could arrive at eternal life. And so, wishing to remedy your great evils, I have given you the bridge of My Son, so that you may pass across the flood—the tempestuous sea of this dark life—and not be drowned. See, therefore, under what obligation the creature is to me, and how ignorant he is not to take the remedy that I have offered, but to be willing to drown."

Thank You, Christ, for saving me.

APRIL 5

The LORD is God and has enlightened us. Join in procession
with leafy branches up to the horns of the altar.
—Psalm 118:27 (NAB)

"I have seen so many souls, seduced by [a] false light, flying like poor butterflies and burning their wings, then coming back toward the true, the sweet light of love that gave them new wings, more brilliant and light, so that they might fly toward Jesus, that Divine Fire 'who burns without consuming.'"
—St. Thérèse of Lisieux

Holy Spirit, show me Your truth. Bring me close to You, today.

═══ APRIL 6 ═══

$\mathcal{S}$o we do not lose heart. Though our outer self is wasting
away, our inner self is being renewed day by day.
—2 Corinthians 4:16 (ESV)

"The soul becomes nothing other than an altar on which God is
adored in praise and love, and God alone is on it. This is why God
commanded that the altar on which the Ark of the Covenant was
to be laid should be hollow inside: so that the soul may understand how completely empty God desires it to be in order to be
an altar worthy of His majestic presence." —St. John of the Cross

I don't want other things. I want You.

═══ APRIL 7 ═══

"[$\mathcal{W}$]hoever wishes to be great among you must be your
servant." —Matthew 20:26b (NRSV)

"The love that Christ requires is intense. He didn't even stop
at requiring love, but added, 'The Son of Man came not to be
served but to serve, and to give His life a ransom for many' (Matt.
20:28), pointing out that we ought to love even to the point of
being killed for our beloved. For this above all is to love Him. In
the same way, he also says to Peter, 'If you love Me, then feed My
sheep' (cf. John 21:16)." —St. John Chrysostom

Show me today where humility is lacking in my love.

=== APRIL 8 ===

[*B*]e kind to one another, compassionate, forgiving one
another as God has forgiven you in Christ.
—Ephesians 4:32 (NAB)

"Happy are the souls that are loved by [true spiritual friends].
Happy the day on which they came to know them. O my Lord,
will You grant me the favor of giving me many who have such
love for me? Truly, Lord, I would rather be loved by these than
by all the kings of the world, for such friends use every means
in their power to give us dominion over the whole world and
to have all that is in the world subject to us. Love such persons
as much as you like. There can be very few of them, but it is the
Lord's will that their goodness should be known. When you are
striving for perfection, you will be told that you don't need to
know such people; it is enough for you to know God. But, to
get to know God's friends is a very good way of getting to know
Him." —St. Teresa of Avila

Thank You for the friends You've sent my way.

=== APRIL 9 ===

[*J*esus said,] "For if you forgive others their trespasses, your
heavenly Father will also forgive you." —Matthew 6:14 (NRSV)

"Someone in a monastery was falsely accused of sexual sins, and
he arose and went to see Antony. The brothers also came from

the monastery to correct him and take him back. They tried to prove that he had done this thing, but he defended himself and denied that he had done anything of the kind. Now Cephalus happened to be there and he told this parable: 'I have seen a man on the bank of the river buried up to his knees in mud, and some men came to give him a hand to help him out. But they pushed him further in up to his neck.' Then Antony said this about Cephalus: 'Here is a real man, who can care for souls and save them.' Everyone there was pierced to the heart by Antony's words, and they asked the brother's forgiveness. So, scolded by the fathers, they took the brother back to the monastery."

—*The Wisdom of the Desert Fathers and Mothers*

Quiet my judgmental mind, today, Lord.

═══ **APRIL 10** ═══

[*B*]e renewed in the spirit of your minds, and put
on the new self, created in God's way in
righteousness and holiness of truth.
—Ephesians 4:23–24 (NAB)

"The Holy Spirit is the light with which God lights our path and directs us toward sanctification, and on this path we follow the Son. The spiritual experience becomes nothing other than our response in faith, hope, and love to God the Father, who addresses to each of us, in baptism, the words that reveal our identity: 'You are My son,' or 'You are My daughter.' Sons and daughters in Jesus Christ the Son: this is the promise and the path revealed to us in baptism!" —Enzo Bianchi

Lead me, Holy Spirit. I need Your light.

=== APRIL 11 ===

*G*racious is the LORD and righteous; yes, our God is merciful.
—Psalm 116:5 (NAB)

"If I understand rightly, supreme and eternal Truth, I am the thief and you have been punished for me. For I see your Word, your Son, fastened and nailed to the cross. Of him you have made a Bridge for me, your miserable servant. For this reason, my heart is bursting, and yet cannot burst, through the hunger and the desire that it has conceived toward You." —St. Catherine of Siena

I will rest in God's mercy today.

=== APRIL 12 ===

*T*he LORD protects the simple; I was helpless, but he saved me.
—Psalm 116:6 (NAB)

"For a long time I wondered why God showed partiality; why all souls don't receive the same amount of graces. I was astounded to see Him lavish extraordinary favors on the Saints who had offended Him, such as St. Paul and St. Augustine, and whom He so to speak forced to receive His graces. Or when I read the life of Saints whom our Lord was pleased to embrace from the cradle to the grave, without leaving in their path any obstacles that might hinder them from rising toward Him, and granting these souls such favors that they were unable to tarnish the immaculate brightness of their baptismal robes, I wondered why poor primitive people, for example, were dying in great numbers without even having heard the name of God pronounced."

—St. Thérèse of Lisieux [continued tomorrow . . .]

Your grace astounds me, especially when I know that I offend You.

══ APRIL 13 ══

$\mathcal{C}$ultivate inner beauty, the gentle, gracious
kind that God delights in.
—1 Peter 3:4 (The Message)

St. Thérèse of Lisieux continues her reflection from yesterday: "Jesus consented to teach me this mystery. He placed before my eyes the book of nature; I understood that all the flowers that He created are beautiful. The brilliance of the rose and the whiteness of the lily don't take away the perfume of the lowly violet or the delightful simplicity of the daisy. I understood that if all the little flowers wanted to be roses, nature would lose its springtime adornment, and the fields would no longer be sprinkled with little flowers. So it is in the world of souls, which is Jesus' garden. He wanted to create great saints who could be compared to lilies and roses. But He also created little ones, and these ought to be content to be daisies or violets destined to gladden God's eyes when He glances down at His feet. Perfection consists in doing His will, in being what He wants us to be."

If St. Thérèse considered herself a "Little Flower" for You, so am I content to be. Thank You, God.

═══ APRIL 14 ═══

*Beloved, do not believe every spirit, but test
the spirits to see whether they are from God; for many
false prophets have gone out into the world.
By this you know the Spirit of God.*
—1 John 4:1–2a (NRSV)

"Great harm is done to the beauty of the soul by its unruly desires for the things of this world. Although it is true that in its created being the soul is as perfect as when God created it, yet in its unruly being it is vile, abominable, and full of many evils. A single unruly desire is enough to bring a soul into such vileness that it cannot come into union with God until the desire is purified." —St. John of the Cross

Holy Father, steer me away from what denies You, today.

APRIL 15

*Y*ou anoint my head with oil; my cup overflows.
—Psalm 23:5b (NAB)

"There are people whose nature is very much affected by small things. If you are not like this, do not neglect to have compassion on others. It may be that our Lord wishes to spare us these sufferings and give us sufferings of another kind that will seem heavy to us, though to others they may seem light. In these matters, we must not judge others by ourselves nor think of ourselves at some time when the Lord has made us stronger than they. Let us think about what we were like at the times when we have been the weakest." —St. Teresa of Avila

I know that You are caring for me, no matter what happens.

APRIL 16

*G*oodness and mercy will pursue me all the days of my life; I will dwell in the house of the LORD for endless days.
—Psalm 23:6 (NAB)

"St. Antony once said, 'I no longer fear God, but I love Him. For love casts out fear.'"
—*The Wisdom of the Desert Fathers and Mothers*

I want to really know You, God. I don't want to be afraid.

𝒷efore I formed you in the womb I knew you,
before you were born I set you apart.
—Jeremiah 1:5a (NIV)

"I have no merit in not having given myself over to the love of created things, since I was preserved from this only by God's great mercy! I recognize that without Him, I would have fallen as low as Mary Magdalene did, and the profound words of Our Lord to Simon echo with great sweetness in my soul. I know, 'Whoever has been forgiven little, loves little' [Lk. 7:47], but I also know that Jesus has forgiven me more than He did for Mary Magdalene, since He forgave me in advance, keeping me from falling." —St. Thérèse of Lisieux

I may not be the greatest sinner, God, but I cling to Your forgiveness all the same!

═ **APRIL 18** ═

𝒯he LORD is my light and my salvation; whom should I fear?
—Psalm 27:1a (NAB)

"Every day you give yourself to us, representing Yourself in the sacrament of the altar, in the body of Your holy Church. What has done this? Your mercy. Oh, divine mercy! My heart suffocates in thinking of You, for everywhere I turn my thoughts, I find nothing but mercy. Eternal Father! Forgive my ignorance

that makes me presume to chatter to You. The love of Your mercy will be my excuse before the face of Your loving-kindness."
—St. Catherine of Siena

I will rest for a moment in the Father's love. I will pause and remember Christ's mercy.

═══ APRIL 19 ═══

*H*ear my voice, LORD, when I call; have
mercy on me and answer me.
—Psalm 27:7 (NAB)

"God's spark can find us in any situation, circumstance, or event. Some experiences are powerfully positive: a weekend retreat, the birth of a child, an uplifting worship service, a heart-to-heart conversation with a trusted friend, someone's profession of love for us, or the sight of a beautiful sunset. Sometimes a catalyst is painful: a loved one's death, the diagnosis of a disease, the loss of a home in a natural disaster, or being laid off from work. In either case, this experience of grace is unique to each person and tailored to his or her season and situation. The circumstances are limitless, since nothing is impossible for God (see Luke 1:37)."
—Fr. Albert Haase, OFM

Is there a loss or painful experience that is prompting me to change something about my life?

APRIL 20

"Come," says my heart, "seek his face"; your face,
Lord, do I seek!"
—Psalm 27:8 (NAB)

"For the soul to come to unite itself perfectly with God through love and will, it must first be free from all desire of the will, however slight. It must not intentionally and knowingly consent with the will to imperfections, and it must have power and freedom to be able not so to consent intentionally. The soul will eventually reach the stage of not even having these desires, for they develop out of a habit of imperfection." —St. John of the Cross

**Give me strength today to do what I should do,
and to not do what I know I shouldn't do.**

APRIL 21

[The disciples] did not understand what he said to them. . . .
His mother treasured all these things in her heart.
—Luke 2:50–51 (NRSV)

"The final space of prayer is death, in which every human being gives his soul back to God. Thus it comes as no surprise that, after the Our Father, the best known Christian prayer is the Hail Mary, which concludes: 'Holy Mary, Mother of God, pray for us sinners now and in the hour of our death.' These words, which believing parents teach their children, in fact are rich in hope, communicating not only that we are all destined to die, but that, thank God, we will not die alone. Notwithstanding the sins we may have committed, there is someone who will pray for us: a holy woman, mother of a Son who was without sin yet who died; a woman who now lives in her Son's risen glory and prays that we too may reach that place." —Timothy Verdon

Pray for me, Holy Mother of God.

=== **APRIL 22** ===

My soul yearns and pines for the courts of the LORD.
—Psalm 84:3a (NAB)

"Keep phrases like 'My life!' 'My love!' and 'My darling!' for your Spouse [Jesus Christ], for you will be so often alone with Him that you will want to use them all. If you use them among yourselves, they will not move the Lord so much." —St. Teresa of Avila

You are my love, my life, O Lord.

=== **APRIL 23** ===

Do not be conformed to this world, but be transformed by the renewal of your mind, that by testing you may discern what is the will of God, what is good and acceptable and perfect.
—Romans 12:2 (ESV)

"The key to living in the here and now is awareness of what we are doing and acceptance of what is going on beyond the surface of appearances. This daily discipline is difficult and takes practice. It requires that we be sensitive to what we are experiencing, accept the person before us without judgment, savor and enjoy what surrounds us, and deal with interruptions and change of plans with grace and peace. When we live fully in the here and now, we reverence the holiness of each action of our daily routine. Why? Because we are convinced that this moment is God's ambassador that reveals the divine will for us in the here and now. Generously accepting the present moment, we can then gratefully bow to receive its blessing." —Sr. Bridget Haase, OSU

Is there anything keeping me from living in the here and now, today?

═══ APRIL 24 ═══

A Samaritan woman came to draw water, and
Jesus said to her, "Give me a drink."
—John 4:7 (NRSV)

"God is with those who love Him: in the context of real situations and in the light of everyday duties, He draws near and asks things to which He has a right. We pray to Him, but He too, in a certain sense, prays to us, saying 'Give Me to drink.' And He lets us know that the One asking this favor can make springs well up in the soul that gives Him what He wants, waters of life eternal." —Timothy Verdon

What can I do for You today, Most High?

APRIL 25

*T*he human mind plans the way,
but the LORD directs the steps.
—Proverbs 16:9 (NRSV)

Christ spoke to St. Catherine of Siena: "You are free agents. As such, you can hold onto your free will or leave it, according as you please. It is a weapon that, if you place it in the hands of the devil, immediately becomes a knife with which he strikes you and slays you."

I can say "no" or "yes" to You. Yes!

APRIL 26

*M*ay you be made strong with all the strength that comes
from his glorious power, and may you be prepared to
endure everything with patience, while joyfully giving
thanks to the Father, who has enabled you to share in the
inheritance of the saints in the light.
—Colossians 1:11–12 (NRSV)

"Here's an example that will interpret my thoughts a little: Suppose that the son of a capable doctor encounters on the road a rock that makes him fall, and that as a result of this fall he breaks a limb. Immediately his father comes to him, picks him up lovingly, takes care of his wounds, and in so doing uses all the resources of his art, and soon his son, now completely healed, bears witness to his gratitude. Without any doubt, this son is quite right to love his father!" —St. Thérèse of Lisieux [continued tomorrow . . .]

God, thank You for picking me up when I fall.

═══ APRIL 27 ═══

The LORD *is my shepherd.*
—Psalm 23:1a (NAB)

[Continued from yesterday] "But I'm going to make still another supposition. The father, knowing that on the road his son was taking there was a rock, hurries to go before him and removes it (without anybody seeing him). Certainly, this son, the object of the father's prevenient tenderness, not KNOWING the misfortune from which he's been delivered by his father, won't bear witness of his gratitude, and will love him less than if he had been cured by him. But if he comes to know the danger that he has just escaped, will he not love him more? Well, I am this child who is the object of the anticipatory love of a Father who sent His Word not to redeem the righteous but sinners. He wants me to love Him because He has forgiven me, not much, but everything." —St. Thérèse of Lisieux

God, thank You for picking me up even before I fall!

APRIL 28

" *Is* not my word like fire," declares the LORD, "and
like a hammer that breaks a rock in pieces?"
—Jeremiah 23:29 (NIV)

"Antony said, 'Whoever hammers a lump of iron, first decides
what he is going to make from it. Even so we ought to make up
our minds what kind of virtue we want to forge, or we labor in
vain.'" —*The Wisdom of the Desert Fathers and Mothers*

**I will consider today what virtue I most of all need to cultivate. I
will pray to God with my intention.**

APRIL 29

Today is the Feast Day of St. Catherine of Siena

"Fire of Love! Thanks, thanks be to You, eternal Father!
I am imperfect and full of darkness, and You, perfection and
   light,
have shown to me perfection and the resplendent way of the
doctrine of Your only-begotten Son.
I was dead, and You have brought Me to life.
I was sick, and You have given Me medicine."
—A prayer of St. Catherine of Siena

Thank You for bringing me to life.

[T]he first step in learning is bowing down to GOD; only fools
thumb their noses at such wisdom and learning.
—Proverbs 1:7 (THE MESSAGE)

"How inappropriate it is for me to begin to praise humility and
sacrifice when these virtues are so highly praised by the King of
Glory, a praise exemplified in all the trials He suffered. You must
work to possess these virtues, my daughters, if you are to leave
the land of Egypt. For when you have attained these virtues, you
will also attain the manna. All things will taste good to you, and
no matter how much the world may dislike their savor, to you
they will be sweet." —St. Teresa of Avila

Teach me humility and sacrifice, today.

May

== MAY 1 ==

[I] will proclaim your name to my brethren;
in the assembly I will praise you.
—Psalm 22:23 (NAB)

"I have said that St. Francis deliberately did not see the wood for the trees. It is even more true that he deliberately did not see the mob for the men. What distinguishes this very genuine democrat from any mere demagogue is that he never either deceived or was deceived by the illusion of mass-suggestion. Whatever his taste in monsters, he never saw before him a many-headed beast. He only saw the image of God multiplied but never monotonous." —G. K. Chesterton

Help me today to see every person in the image of You.

== MAY 2 ==

Who may go up the mountain of the LORD?
Who can stand in his holy place?
—Psalm 24:3 (NAB)

God once spoke to St. Catherine of Siena, saying, "The soul, by its nature, always relishes good, though it is true that the soul, blinded by self-love, does not always know and discern what is true good and profitable to the soul and to the body."

Lord, show me what is truly good. Reveal what's bad, so I'm not fooled.

═══ MAY 3 ═══

*B*ut if God himself has taken up residence in your life, you can hardly be thinking more of yourself than of him. Anyone, of course, who has not welcomed this invisible but clearly present God, the Spirit of Christ, won't know what we're talking about.
—Romans 8:9 (THE MESSAGE)

"God will never force or put pressure upon us; with utmost respect for human free will, all God can do is invite us, encourage us, nudge us, and entice us. God tugs at the heart. And God does so through spiritual desires and longings that are placed deep within us." —Fr. Albert Haase, OFM

I feel Your nudge today, Lord. I am here.

═══ MAY 4 ═══

*T*o you, LORD, I call; my Rock, do not be deaf to me.
—Psalm 28:1a (NAB)

"Desire, when it is carried into effect, is sweet and appears to be good, but it tastes bitter afterwards. The truth of this can be clearly proved by anyone who allows himself to be led away by it. Yet there are some persons so blind and insensible as not to feel

this, for as they do not walk in God, they are unable to perceive what hinders them from approaching Him."
—St. John of the Cross

**Sometimes my desire for You feels unrequited.
I just want You to know that.**

═══ MAY 5 ═══

By this we know that we abide in him and he in us,
because he has given us of his Spirit.
—1 John 4:13 (NRSV)

"We must therefore be steadily committed to this way of life with God as our helper, for it is written: 'We know that all things work together for good for those who love God' (Rom. 8:28). Let us reflect on the apostle's claim that he dies each day, so that we can avoid idleness. If we bear in mind the unpredictability of our human condition, we will not sin. For when we wake from sleep, we are unsure whether we will reach evening, and when we lie down to rest at night, we should not be confident that daylight will return. We should be aware always of the uncertainty of our life and know that we are governed by God's providence."
—St. Antony, as told by St. Athanasius

**Remind me how brief life is, Lord, and how
important my every action can be.**

═══ MAY 6 ═══

*H*ope deferred makes the heart sick, but a
desire fulfilled is a tree of life.
—Proverbs 13:12 (NRSV)

"St. Gregory the Theologian once said, 'These three things God requires of all the baptized: right faith in the heart, truth on the tongue, and temperance in the body.' He also said, 'The entire life of humankind is but one single day for those who are working hard with longing.'"
—*The Wisdom of the Desert Fathers and Mothers*

I want You, Lord. I want You.

═══ MAY 7 ═══

[*J*esus said,] "There's nothing they can do to your soul,
your core being. Save your fear for God, who holds
your entire life—body and soul—in his hands."
—Matthew 10:28b (THE MESSAGE)

"We must first rid ourselves immediately of our love for our bodies. Some of us pamper ourselves so much that doing so will be hard work. It is also amazing how concerned some of us are about having a healthy body. Some of us think, though, that we embraced the religious life for no other reason than to keep ourselves alive. In our community, there is very little chance for us to act on such a principle. We have come here to die for Christ, not

to practice self-indulgence for Christ. The devil tells us that we need to be self-indulgent if we are to keep the Rule of our Order. So many of us try to keep the Rule by looking after our health that we die without having kept it for even a day."
—St. Teresa of Avila

Teach me today when I need to ignore myself in order to see You.

═══ MAY 8 ═══

[Jesus said,] "When people realize it is the living God you are presenting and not some idol that makes them feel good, they are going to turn on you, even people in your own family. There is a great irony here: proclaiming so much love, experiencing so much hate! But don't quit. Don't cave in. It is all well worth it in the end. It is not success you are after in such times but survival. Be survivors! Before you've run out of options, the Son of Man will have arrived."
—Matthew 10:21–23 (THE MESSAGE)

"I've heard it said that there is no pure soul that can be found who loves more than a repentant soul. Oh! how I would like to believe that saying!" —St. Thérèse of Lisieux

I need You, God, now more than ever.

I cried out to you for help and you healed me.
—Psalm 30:3b (NAB)

God spoke to St. Catherine of Siena: "Do you know what is the special good of the blessed ones? It is having their desire filled with what they desire. So you see that My servants are blessed principally in seeing and in knowing Me. In this vision and knowledge their will is fulfilled, for they have what they desire to have, and so they are satisfied."

I desire only You, today, Lord!

If I give away all my possessions, and if I hand over my body
so that I may boast, but do not have love, I gain nothing.
—1 Corinthians 13:3 (NRSV)

"Let's sketch out what this virtue of love really is, since it can be so difficult to actually see in the world. Let's consider how great the benefits would be if it were everywhere in abundance—how there would be no need for laws or tribunals or punishments or avenging or any other of those sorts of things, since if all loved and were beloved, no human being would injure another. Think of it! Murders, strife, wars, divisions, plundering, fraud, and all evils would be removed. Vice would become unknown even in

name. If this were to happen, it would be better than miracles."
—St. John Chrysostom

I know that I can love those closest to me, better. Show me how.

=== MAY 11 ===

"For those who want to save their life will lose it,
and those who lose their life for my sake, and for
the sake of the gospel, will save it."
—Mark 8:35 (NRSV)

"Mary prays for us in the hour of our death, but does not pray that we not die. Rather, in the spirit of the words of St. Bonaventure. . . . Mary knows that 'only someone who loves death may see God, for in spite of everything it remains true that "man cannot see Me and live."'. . . it is thus Mary—not only mother of the Crucified but also figure of his Church—who whispers to all who approach the end of life: 'Let us die therefore; let us enter this darkness. Let us silence temptations, worldly desires, fantasies. Let us pass from this world to the Father with Christ crucified, so that, after seeing Him, we can say with Philip: "this is enough for us.""" —Timothy Verdon

Blessed Virgin Mary, pray for me in the hour of my death.

*P*ut to death therefore what is earthly in you:
sexual immorality, impurity, passion, evil desire, and
covetousness, which is idolatry.
—Colossians 3:5 (ESV)

"Father Gerontius said that many, tempted by the pleasures of the body, commit sexual sins, not in their body only but also in their spirit. Thus, while preserving their body's purity, they commit prostitution in their soul. 'Thus it is good, my well-beloved, to do that which is written, and for each one to guard his own heart with all possible care.'"
—*The Wisdom of the Desert Fathers and Mothers*

Remind me of my sins, today, Lord. Don't let me take them lightly.

*T*urn my eyes from looking at worthless things;
and give me life in your ways.
—Psalm 119:37 (ESV)

"While Jesus was alive he desired no other pleasure than to do the will of His Father, which He called His meat and food. So if a person has the opportunity to listen to things that do not honor or serve God, he should not desire to listen to them. So it is with all the senses, insofar as he can fairly avoid the pleasure in question. If he cannot, it is enough that he wills not to take pleasure in this thing." —St. John of the Cross

I will pay close attention to what I listen to today.

═ MAY 14 ═

*W*hen Daniel learned that the decree had been signed and
posted, he continued to pray just as he had always done.
His house had windows in the upstairs that opened toward
Jerusalem. Three times a day he knelt there in prayer,
thanking and praising his God.
—Daniel 6:10 (THE MESSAGE)

"It is really amusing to see how some people torture themselves. . . . Sometimes they perform penances without any reason. They perform them for a few days and then the devil puts it into their heads that they have been doing themselves harm and makes them afraid of penances. After this they don't . . . keep the smallest points in the Rule, such as silence, which is quite incapable of harming them. If we imagine we have a headache, we stay away from choir. One day we are absent because we had a headache some time ago. Another day we are absent because our head has just begun to ache again. We are absent the next three days in case it aches any more. Then we want to invent penances on our own, and we end up doing neither one thing nor the other. Sometimes there is very little wrong with us, but we think it should release us from all our obligations." —St. Teresa of Avila

I'm tired, but I still want to praise You.

"[t]he last will be first, and the first will be last."
—Matthew 20:16 (NRSV)

"God's patience and generosity are magnanimous. That's why spiritual thoughts or feelings suddenly like flying sparks arise out of nowhere and keep recurring. They are indications of God's insistent determination to have a relationship with us. Jesus's parable of the workers in the vineyard (cf. Matt. 20:1–16) speaks to this. A landowner goes out at various hours and hires day laborers to work in his vineyard. At the end of the day, when the landowner pays them, the laborers who worked only an hour received the same per diem as those hired at the beginning of the day. Jesus does not say the late hires received a full day's pay because they worked hard and gave it their all but because the landowner is 'generous' (cf. v. 15)." —Fr. Albert Haase, OFM

**In what aspect of life do I see God persistently
trying to get my attention?**

The voice of the LORD strikes with fiery flame;
the voice of the LORD shakes the desert.
—Psalm 29:7–8a (NAB)

God said to St. Catherine of Siena, "How do people have the pledge of eternal life in the present? They have it by seeing My goodness in themselves, and by knowing My truth. Their intellect (which is the eye of the soul), illuminated in Me, possesses My truth. This eye has the pupil of the most holy faith, the light of which enables the soul to discern, to know, and to follow the way and the doctrine of My Truth—the Word incarnate."

Show me Your truth, today, Lord.

$=$ **MAY 17** $=$

I belong to my beloved.
—Song of Song 7:10a (NIV)

"[God] wants me to love Him because He has forgiven me, not much, but everything. He didn't wait for me to love Him much like Mary Magdalene, but He wanted ME TO KNOW how much He loved me with an inexpressible anticipation, so that now I might love Him to distraction!" —St. Thérèse of Lisieux

I want to learn to love You "to distraction," forsaking all else.

$=$ **MAY 18** $=$

As the deer longs for streams of water,
so my soul longs for you, O God.
—Psalm 42:2 (NAB)

"Faith leads us to a *genuine experience* of God: in other words, it introduces us to spiritual life, which is life guided by the Holy Spirit. Anyone who believes in God also needs to experience God—correct ideas about God are not enough. The experience of God, which always takes place in a context of faith and not sight (cf. 2 Cor. 5:7: 'We walk by faith, not by sight'), is an experience whose authenticity startles us. We find ourselves repeating with Jacob, 'The Lord is in this place—and I did not know it!' (Gen. 28:16), or with the Psalmist, 'You hem me in, behind and before. . . . Where can I flee from your presence? If I ascend to heaven, you are there; if I make my bed in Sheol, you are there' (Ps. 139:5, 7-8)." —Enzo Bianchi

I know You are in this place.

═ MAY 19 ═

*M*ay you be made strong with all the strength that
comes from his glorious power, and may you
be prepared to endure everything with patience. . . .
—Colossians 1:11 (NRSV)

"We are also children of hope with master plans. But the future is both a challenge and a mystery. Until it is upon us, it keeps the secret of all the crossroads and detours of our journeys. We can never be sure when the earth will shift under our feet, when our goals will sway, or our dreams totter. But nurturing hope always grounds and sustains us. It opens us to potential and possibility, fosters undying dreams, stirs up passion for what lies ahead, and keeps us putting one foot in front of the other."

—Sr. Bridget Haase, OSU

Nurture my hope, Lord. I want to be surprised by Your grace.

You shall also love the stranger, for you were
strangers in the land of Egypt.
—Deuteronomy 10:19 (NRSV)

"There was in the monasteries an old man called Apollo. . . . When he taught about how to welcome others, Apollo said that one should bow before the brothers who come. We should do this since it is God, not the brothers themselves, before whom we are bowing. 'When you see your brother,' he said, 'you see the Lord your God.' He added, 'We have learned that from Abraham (cf. Genesis 18). When you receive the brothers, invite them to rest awhile, for this is what we learn from Lot, who invited the angels to do so.'" —*The Wisdom of the Desert Fathers and Mothers*

**I will look for an opportunity today to welcome a
stranger into my life.**

To this you were called, because Christ suffered for you,
leaving you an example, that you should follow in his steps.
—1 Peter 2:21 (NIV)

"Our body has one fault: the more you indulge it, the more things
it discovers that it has to have. It is extraordinary how the body
likes to be indulged. If there is any reasonable pretext for indulgence, no matter how unnecessary it is, the poor soul is taken
in and prevented from making progress. Think about how many
poor people must be ill and have no one to complain to. . . . Surely
we have not come here to indulge ourselves. . . . You are free from
the great trials of the world. Learn to suffer a little for the love of
God without telling everyone about it. . . . Can't we . . . keep secret
between God and us some of the afflictions he sends us because
of our sins? After all, talking about them does not help to lessen
them." —St. Teresa of Avila

My "suffering" is nothing compared to Your love.

That's why we live with such good cheer. You won't see
us drooping our heads or dragging our feet! Cramped
conditions here don't get us down. They only remind us of
the spacious living conditions ahead. It's what we trust in but
don't yet see that keeps us going. Do you suppose a few ruts

in the road or rocks in the path are going to stop us?
When the time comes, we'll be plenty ready to
exchange exile for homecoming.
—2 Corinthians 5:6–8 (THE MESSAGE)

"Imaginative identification with Christ's paschal mystery prepares Christians first to live and then to die well. For both of these goals we in fact need 'skill,' 'craftsmanship,' because— according to biblical wisdom—'there is a season for everything, a time for every occupation under heaven: a time for giving birth, a time for dying; a time for planting, a time for uprooting what has been planted' (Eccl. 3:1–2). That is why the Church surrounds [death] with significant rituals, carefully defining moments and modalities. With words and eloquent gestures she teaches that death, for Christians, is above all a *birth*." —Timothy Verdon

God, may I be ready for death, that new birth, when it comes.

═ MAY 23 ═

$\mathscr{H}$e has told you, O mortal, what is good; and what does
the LORD require of you but to do justice, and to love
kindness, and to walk humbly with your God?
—Micah 6:8 (NRSV)

"Strive to go about seeking not the best of temporal things, but the worst. Strive so to desire to enter into complete detachment

from the world, and emptiness and poverty with respect to everything that is in the world, for Christ's sake."
—St. John of the Cross

How is God asking me to be poor for Him?

$=$ MAY 24 $=$

*R*everently respect GOD, your God, serve him, hold tight to him, back up your promises with the authority of his name.
He's your praise! He's your God!
—Deuteronomy 10:20 (THE MESSAGE)

God spoke to St. Catherine of Siena: "The pupil of the intellect is faith. If the soul has covered faith with the cloth of infidelity, drawn over it by self-love, it does not see. It has only the form of the eye without the light, because it has hidden the pupil. Thus you see that in seeing, my servants know, and in knowing, they love, and in loving, they deny and lose their self-will. Their own will now lost, they clothe themselves in My will."

Give me more faith, Lord. Bless my desire for You.

*B*eloved, let us love one another, for love is from God, and whoever loves has been born of God and knows God. Anyone who does not love does not know God, because God is love.
—1 John 4:7–8 (ESV)

"Oh! How much compassion I feel for souls who are becoming lost! It's so easy to wander off onto the flowery paths of the world. No doubt . . . the sweetness that it offers is mixed with bitterness and the immense emptiness of the desires could never be filled by the praises of a moment." —St. Thérèse of Lisieux

Shine a light for me, Christ, so that I will not stray from Your path.

*S*o let's *do* it—full of belief, confident that we're presentable inside and out. Let's keep a firm grip on the promises that keep us going. He always keeps his word. Let's see how inventive we can be in encouraging love and helping out, not avoiding worshiping together as some do but spurring each other on, especially as we see the big Day approaching.
—Hebrews 10:22–25 (THE MESSAGE)

"Spiritual transformation is not meant to be a solitary, individual affair; nor is it done in isolation from the world. It stretches the heart beyond the ego—'from me to thee,' as a wise spiritual director once told me. Becoming a little Christ involves selfless love and service. This is learned within a community of flesh-and-blood believers who 'wash each other's feet,' learn to forgive each other, celebrate life events as sacramental moments, and welcome to their table the poor, the sinner, and the marginalized. Christianity without community is a caricature."

—Fr. Albert Haase, OFM

The next time I go to Mass, I will look at my neighbors in a new way.

═══ MAY 27 ═══

[*Jesus said,*] "Do not judge, so that you may not be judged."
—Matthew 7:1 (NRSV)

"Someone once questioned Father Poemen: 'My thoughts often disturb me, making me put my sins aside. My thoughts are then occupied with my brother's faults.' The old man told him the following story about Father Dioscorus: 'In his room he wept over himself, while his disciple was sitting in another prayer chamber. When the latter came to see the old man he asked him, "Father, why are you weeping?" "I am weeping over my sins," the old man answered him. Then his disciple said, "You do not have any sins, Father." The old man replied, "Truly, my child, if I were allowed to see my sins, three or four people would not be enough to weep for them."'" —*The Wisdom of the Desert Fathers and Mothers*

Father, I will not think of my neighbor's sins. I won't! I have enough of my own.

$\mathcal{D}$o you not know that in a race the runners all
compete, but only one receives the prize?
Run in such a way that you may win it.
—1 Corinthians 9:24 (NRSV)

"Let us remember our holy Fathers, the hermits, whose lives we strive to imitate. What sufferings, solitude, cold, and burning heat, and hunger and thirst they bore. Yet they had no one to complain to except God. Do you think they were made of iron? They were as frail as we are. Once we begin to subdue these miserable bodies of ours, they give us much less trouble. There will be plenty of people to see to what you really need. Do not think about yourselves except when you know it is necessary."
—St. Teresa of Avila

**I sometimes feel so frail. What a blessing it is
to know that You know that.**

[$\mathcal{J}$esus] said to them, "Pay attention to what you hear;
the measure you give will be the measure you get,
and still more will be given you."
—Mark 4:24 (NRSV)

"The holy man was traveling to a city in India. Running late due to the crowd of onlookers pressing to see him, Mahatma Gandhi was walking quickly to board the train when his sandal loosened, fell off, and landed on the ground. As he paused and bent over to retrieve it, a poor barefooted boy spied the sandal, grabbed it tightly, and ran.

Gandhi boarded the train. Sitting next to a window and glancing out, he noticed the youth looking from afar, waving Gandhi's sandal with a sense of satisfaction and delight. Immediately, Gandhi removed the other one from his foot, aimed it in the direction of the boy, and tossed it out the window. The friend accompanying Gandhi asked why he had done such a thing since they were the only sandals he owned. Gandhi replied with humble compassion, 'Now he has a pair.' Three hours later, the train pulled into a rainy, slippery station and Gandhi disembarked, barefooted." —Sr. Bridget Haase, osu

What may I do for Your people today, Lord? Show me.

MAY 30

"Unquiet Vigil"
by Br. Paul Quenon, ocso

Stale prayer from
unreal depths—
depths I assume are mine—

are relieved by
real sleep,
that awakens me to my

real shallows where
prayer amounts to
almost nothing
or less.

Such an infinity where
almost nothing
dividing endlessly
never reaches
nothing

wherein are
real depths
not mine. . . .

Be kind.
Myself, to myself, be kind.

I will make more time for You, God.

<hr />

═══ MAY 31 ═══

*B*lessed is the man who remains steadfast under trial, for
when he has stood the test he will receive the crown of life,
which God has promised to those who love him.
—James 1:12 (ESV)

As God explained to St. Catherine of Siena: "My servants bear
everything with reverence, deeming themselves favored in having tribulation for My sake, and they desire nothing but what I

desire. If I allow the devil to trouble them, permitting tempta-tions to prove them in virtue, they resist with their will fortified in Me."

Thank You for giving me strength.

June

JUNE 1

*M*y soul thirsts for God, the living God.
—Psalm 42:3a (NAB)

"I knew how to speak to [Christ] alone. Conversations with created beings, even pious conversations, tired out my soul. I felt that it was better to talk to God rather than to talk about God, because so much pride gets mixed into spiritual conversations!"
—St. Thérèse of Lisieux

I re-commit myself to talk with You each day.

JUNE 2

[*J*esus said,] "[G]ive, and it will be given to you. A good measure, pressed down, shaken together, running over, will be put into your lap; for the measure you give will be the measure you get back."
—Luke 6:38 (NRSV)

"[St. Francis of Assisi] honored all men; that is, he not only loved but respected them all. What gave him his extraordinary personal power was this; that from the Pope to the beggar, from the sultan of Syria in his pavilion to the ragged robbers crawling out of the wood, there was never a man who looked into those brown burning eyes without being certain that Francis Bernardone was really interested in him." —G. K. Chesterton

God, I'm no saint, but show me how to show Your love to friends and strangers, today.

JUNE 3

$\mathcal{L}$et what you heard from the beginning abide in you.
—1 John 2:24a (NRSV)

"Try not to fear illness and death and commit yourselves to God. What does it matter if we die? How many times have our bodies ridiculed us? Shouldn't we occasionally ridicule them? If we make this resolution day by day, by the grace of the Lord we will be able to control our body. To conquer such an enemy is a great achievement in the battle of life. May the Lord grant, as he is able, that we may do this. I am quite sure that everyone who enjoys such a victory, which I believe is a great one, will understand the advantages it brings. No one will regret having endured trials in order to attain this tranquility and self-mastery."
—St. Teresa of Avila

Christ, help me conquer the enemy in my life.

JUNE 4

$\mathcal{F}$or now we see in a mirror, dimly,
but then we will see face to face.
Now I know only in part;
then I will know fully, even as I have been fully known.
—1 Corinthians 13:12 (NRSV)

Three fathers used to go and visit Antony every year. Two of them used to discuss their thoughts and the salvation of their souls with him, but the third always remained silent and did not ask any questions. After a long time, Antony said to him, "You often come here to see me, but you never ask me anything." The other replied, "It is enough for me to see you, Father."

—*The Wisdom of the Desert Fathers and Mothers*

Let me see You in others.

═══ JUNE 5 ═══

𝒯he wise counsel GOD gives when I'm awake is confirmed by my sleeping heart. Day and night I'll stick with GOD; I've got a good thing going and I'm not letting go. Now you've got my feet on the life path, all radiant from the shining of your face.
Ever since you took my hand, I'm on the right way.

—Psalm 16:7–8, 11 (THE MESSAGE)

"However dark a night may be, something can always be seen. But in true darkness nothing can be seen. In the night of the senses there still remains some light, for the understanding and reason remain and are not blinded. This spiritual night, which is faith, deprives the soul of everything, both as to understanding and as to sense. . . . The less the soul works with its own ability, the more securely it journeys, because it journeys more in faith."

—St. John of the Cross

Give me faith. Give me faith.

JUNE 6

Quick, GOD, I need your helping hand! The last decent
person just went down, all the friends I depended on gone.
Everyone talks in lie language; lies slide off their oily lips. They
doubletalk with forked tongues.
—Psalm 12:1–2 (THE MESSAGE)

"Father Doulas said, 'If the enemy persuades us to give up our
inner peace, we must not listen to him. For nothing is equal to
this peace and the lack of food. These two join together to fight
the enemy. They make interior vision keen.' He also said, 'Detach
yourself from the love of the multitude unless you want your
enemy to question your spirit and trouble your inner peace.'"
—*The Wisdom of the Desert Fathers and Mothers*

**Help me remained focused on You, Lord,
and not the praise of others.**

JUNE 7

[*W*]hatever is true, whatever is honorable, whatever is
just, whatever is pure, whatever is pleasing, whatever is
commendable, if there is any excellence and if there is anything
worthy of praise, think about these things.
—Philippians 4:8 (NRSV)

God spoke to St. Catherine of Siena: "All labor in this life is small,
because time is short. Time is as the point of a needle and no

more, and when time has passed, labor is ended. . . . [The faithful] endure with patience, and the thorns they pass through do not touch their heart, because their heart is drawn out of them and united to Me by the affection of love."

I want my labor in this life to be meaningful.

═══ JUNE 8 ═══

$\mathcal{O}$ Lord, all my longing is before you; my sighing
is not hidden from you.
—Psalm 38:9 (ESV)

"Sometimes I felt that I was alone, quite alone. As during the days of my life as a resident in the boarding school, when I would walk, sad and ill, in the big courtyard, I would repeat these words that always brought peace again and strength in my heart: 'Life is your ship and not your dwelling!' Even when I was quite little these words used to give me courage. And still, now, in spite of the years that have caused so many impressions of childish piety to disappear, the picture of the ship still charms my soul and helps it endure exile." —St. Thérèse of Lisieux [continued tomorrow . . .]

When I feel lonely, I'm reminded that You are my only dwelling.

JUNE 9

$\mathcal{T}$hen the just will be glad; they will rejoice before God;
they will celebrate with great joy.
—Psalm 68:4 (NAB)

[Continued from yesterday] "Doesn't Wisdom also say that 'Life is like a vessel that ploughs through the troubled waves and leaves after it no trace of its rapid passage' [cf. Wis. 5:10]? When I think about these things, my soul plunges into infinity and seems to me already to touch the everlasting shore. It seems to me to receive Jesus' embraces." —St. Thérèse of Lisieux

**When my life feels lost at sea, I at least know
that You are with me.**

JUNE 10

$\mathcal{W}$e thank you, God, we give thanks; we call upon your name.
—Psalm 75:2a (NAB)

"We can acquire self-sacrifice by gradual progress and by never indulging our will and desire, even in small things, and succeed in subduing the body to the spirit. This consists entirely in our ceasing to care about ourselves and our own pleasures, for the least that anyone who is beginning to serve the Lord can offer Him is her life. . . . How do we know that our lives will be so short that they will end only one hour or one moment after we decide to commit our entire service to God? We must not measure

ourselves by anything that comes to an end, least of all by life, since not a day of it is secure. Who, if she thought that each hour might be her last, would not spend it working for God?"
—St. Teresa of Avila

If this were my last day on earth, how would I spend it?

=== JUNE 11 ===

*L*ive by the Spirit . . . and do not gratify the desires of the flesh.
—Galatians 5:16 (NRSV)

"We can become so wrapped up in our achievements and accomplishments that we begin to think we are self-made individuals. We obsess over what people think of us and begin treating those who dislike us as an enemy. Without hesitation, we allow our desires to rule and make decisions about how we should act. We make sure we never run out of food, possessions, and money. Paul refers to the actions associated with these self-centered concerns as the 'works of the flesh' (cf. Galatians 5:19–21)."
—Fr. Albert Haase, OFM

I am nothing without You.

JUNE 12

"I devoutly adore You, hidden Divinity,
truly hidden beneath these figures [the bread and wine]:
My heart submits entirely to You,
and faints as it contemplates You."

—St. Thomas Aquinas's Eucharistic hymn (trans. by Timothy Verdon)

Thank you for Your Presence, O Lord!

JUNE 13

At night I ponder in my heart; and as I meditate,
my spirit probes.
—Psalm 77:6b (NAB)

"One day St. Epiphanius said, 'Reading the Scriptures is a great safeguard against sin.' He also said, 'Ignorance of the Scriptures is at once a steep and dangerous cliff and a deep abyss.'"
—*The Wisdom of the Desert Fathers and Mothers*

I will keep the words of Your Holy Scriptures in my mind and heart today.

$\mathscr{I}$ pray that, according to the riches of his glory, he may grant that you may be strengthened in your inner being with power through his Spirit, and that Christ may dwell in your hearts through faith, as you are being rooted and grounded in love. I pray that you may have the power to comprehend, with all the saints, what is the breadth and length and height and depth, and to know the love of Christ that surpasses knowledge, so that you may be filled with all the fullness of God.
—Ephesians 3:16–19 (NRSV)

"It is quite true that my servants do taste eternal life, receiving the pledge of it in this life. Though they walk on thorns, they are not pricked, because they have known My supreme goodness and searched for it where it was to be found, that is, in the Word, My only-begotten Son."
—St. Catherine of Siena (recording words of God given to her in a vision)

Spending time alone with You is a small piece of heaven.

$\mathscr{N}$ow to him who by the power at work within us is able to accomplish abundantly far more than all we can ask or imagine, to him be glory in the church and in Christ Jesus to all generations, forever and ever. Amen.
—Ephesians 3:20–21 (NRSV)

"I tell you, such a person will live on earth as if it were heaven, everywhere enjoying a kind of serenity, and weaving for himself innumerable crowns! Such a person will keep his own soul pure from envy, wrath, jealousy, pride, vanity, evil lusts, every profane love, and every bad temper. I tell you, even as no one would consciously injure himself, so too, neither would such a person who loves like this ever desire to injure his neighbors. The loving person shall stand with Gabriel himself even while he walks on earth. This is the profile of one who has love."

—St. John Chrysostom [continued tomorrow . . .]

Make me a more loving person today.

═══ JUNE 16 ═══

[St. Peter said,] "Lord, you know that I love you." [And Jesus replied,] "Feed my lambs," [and] "Tend my sheep."
—John 21:15b–16 (NAB)

[Continued from yesterday] "In contrast [to one who has love], he who works miracles and has perfect knowledge without love, even though he may raise ten thousand from the dead, will not profit much by it if he is broken off from all others and not endeavoring to mix himself up with any of his fellow servants. For no other cause than this did Christ say that the sign of perfect love toward Himself is loving one's neighbors."

—St. John Chrysostom

I need new ways to love my neighbors, Lord. Show me.

$\mathcal{N}$o temptation has overtaken you that is not common to man. God is faithful, and he will not let you be tempted beyond your ability, but with the temptation he will also provide the way of escape, that you may be able to endure it.
—1 Corinthians 10:13 (ESV)

"Be careful about your inner thoughts, especially if they have to do with rank. May God, by His Passion, keep us from dwelling upon such thoughts as: 'But I am her senior'; 'But I am older'; 'But I have worked harder'; 'But that other sister is being treated better than I am.' If you have these thoughts, you must quickly stop them. If you allow yourselves to dwell on them, or introduce them into your conversation, they will spread like the plague and in religious houses they may give rise to great abuses. Pray fervently for God's help in this matter." —St. Teresa of Avila

I need Your assistance. My mind goes where I don't want it to go.

=== JUNE 18 ===

$\mathcal{M}$y heart is stirred by a noble theme, as I sing my ode to the king. My tongue is the pen of a nimble scribe.
—Psalm 45:2 (NAB)

"When I remember the past, my soul overflows with gratitude on seeing the favors that I've received from heaven."
—St. Thérèse of Lisieux

Thank You today, God, for . . .

JUNE 19

[Jesus said,] "For truly I tell you, if you have faith the size of a mustard seed, you will say to this mountain, 'Move from here to there,' and it will move; and nothing will be impossible for you."
—Matthew 17:20b (NRSV)

"Faith, the theologians say, is a habit of the soul, certain and obscure. The reason it is an obscure habit is that it makes us believe truths revealed by God Himself that transcend all natural light and exceed all human understanding. For the soul this excessive light of faith that is given to it is thick darkness; it overwhelms greater things and does away with small things, even as the light of the sun overwhelms all other lights. When it shines and disables our visual faculty, other lights do not appear to be lights at all. Even so the light of faith, by its excessive greatness, suppresses and disables the light of the understanding."
—St. John of the Cross

Help me, Lord, develop faith like a habit of the soul.

JUNE 20

Come and see the works of the LORD.
—Psalm 46:9a (NAB)

"At the last, beyond created beauty human beings will behold the beauty of the Creator, contemplating God in Christ Jesus. His alone is the beauty that saves the world."
—Timothy Verdon

**I praise You for the beauty of today, as I wait
for the beauty of Your world to come.**

⸺ JUNE 21 ⸺

*O*n the last day of the festival, the great day, while
Jesus was standing there, he cried out, "Let anyone
who is thirsty come to me, and let the one who believes
in me drink. As the scripture has said, 'Out of the
believer's heart shall flow rivers of living water.'"
—John 7:37–38 (NRSV)

"Whoever follows Christ's doctrine, whether in the most perfect way or by dwelling in the life of common charity, finds the water of life to drink by tasting the fruit of the Blood, through the union of the divine nature with the human nature. And you, finding yourselves in Him, find yourselves also in Me, who am the Sea of Peace, because I am one with Him, and He with Me. So you are invited to the fountain of living water of grace."
—St. Catherine of Siena (recording the words of God given to her in a vision)

I am thirsty, Lord.

"O Caring Christ, I ask You that . . .

When a brother stretches out a hand and calls for help, I may be an answer to his prayer.

When a sister hungers for food or an encouraging, consoling word, I may be an answer to her prayer.

When another is suffering and finds it impossible to pray, I may become his/her pray-er.

When life weighs heavily upon my shoulders and I need another to share my burden, someone may weave a golden thread of care and prayer into my life." —St. Bridget Haase, osu

Your church is all around me, today, Lord.

You are with me; your rod and your staff comfort me.
—Psalm 23:4b (NAB)

"In one sense we are always traveling, and traveling as if we did not know where we were going. In another sense we have already arrived. We cannot arrive at the perfect possession of God in this life, and that is why we are travelling and in darkness. But we already possess Him by grace, and therefore in that sense we have arrived and are dwelling in the light." —Thomas Merton, ocso

I still have so far to go, Lord. Please guide my way.

*O*ne's pride will bring him low, but he who is
lowly in spirit will obtain honor.
—Proverbs 29:23 (esv)

"God deliver us from people who wish to serve Him yet who are
overly concerned with their own honor. Reflect upon how little
they gain from this. The very act of wishing for honor robs us of
it, especially in matters of rank. There is no poison in the world
that is so fatal to perfection." —St. Teresa of Avila

Show me where I am prideful today.

A man without self-control is like a city broken
into and left without walls.
—Proverbs 25:28 (esv)

"I desired the grace 'to have absolute control over my actions, to
be the master and not the slave.' These words from the *Imitation
of Christ* touched me deeply, but I had, so to speak, to purchase,
by my desires, that inestimable grace." —St. Thérèse of Lisieux

**Help me today, Lord, to become the master,
not the slave, of myself.**

[Jesus said,] "Blessed are the poor in spirit,
for theirs is the kingdom of heaven."
—Matthew 5:3 (NRSV)

"Poverty is good and contains within itself all the good things in the world. Those who care nothing for the good things of the world have dominion over all of them. What do kings and lords matter to me if I have no desire for their money, or to please them, if by doing so I displease God? What do their honors mean to me since I have realized that the primary honor of a poor person resides in his being truly poor?"
—St. Teresa of Avila

Lord, above every other thing, I want You.

JUNE 27

Anyone . . .who has not welcomed this invisible but clearly present God, the Spirit of Christ, won't know what we're talking about. But for you who welcome him, in whom he dwells—even though you still experience all the limitations of sin—you yourself experience life on God's terms. It stands to reason, doesn't it, that if the alive-and-present God who raised Jesus from the dead moves into your life, he'll do the same thing in you that he did in Jesus, bringing you alive to himself? When God lives and breathes

in you (and he does, as surely as he did in Jesus), you are delivered from that dead life. With his Spirit living in you, your body will be as alive as Christ's!
—Romans 8:9b–11 (The Message)

～

God spoke to St. Catherine of Siena: "Men and women find peace and quiet when their memories are filled with My love. You know that an empty thing resounds when touched, but not so when it is full. So the memory, being filled with the light of the intellect, and the affection, being filled with love, will not resound with disordinate merriment or with impatience when moved by the tribulations or delights of the world, because they are full of Me, who am every good."

O Lord, fill me today with Your Spirit.

=== **JUNE 28** ===

"From the earliest days of the church, a favored devotion of Christian pilgrims to Jerusalem was to retrace the *via dolorosa*, the 'path of sorrow' that Jesus walked on His journey to Calvary. St. Francis of Assisi is credited with developing the practice of replicating the Way of the Cross by an artistic depiction of its 'stations'—each scene along the final journey of Jesus. You now find Stations of the Cross around the walls of most Catholic churches. Though traditionally set at fourteen, some churches have a fifteenth station representing the Resurrection. Jesus's way of the cross did not end on Calvary; God raised Him up to new life for us all." —Thomas Groome

I will visit a church, today. At each station, I will pause and pray. . . .

We adore You Christ and we praise You, because by Your holy cross You have redeemed the world.

— JUNE 29 —

$\mathscr{I}$ heard a voice out of Heaven, "Write this: Blessed are those who die in the Master from now on; how blessed to die that way!" "Yes," says the Spirit, "and blessed rest from their hard, hard work. None of what they've done is wasted; God blesses them for it all in the end."
—Revelation 14:13 (THE MESSAGE)

"Father Evagrius said, 'Sit in your prayer chamber, collecting your thoughts. Remember the day of your death. See then what the death of your body will be; let your spirit be heavy, take pains, condemn the vanity of the world, so as to be able to live always in the peace you have in view without weakening. Remember also what happens in hell, and think about the state of the souls down there, their painful silence, their most bitter groanings, their fear, their strife, their waiting. Think of their grief without end and the tears their souls shed eternally.'"
—*The Wisdom of the Desert Fathers and Mothers* [continued tomorrow . . .]

I live for You because I know how important my life is.

[Some] will suffer the punishment of eternal destruction,
separated from the presence of the Lord and from the
glory of his might.
—2 Thessalonians 1:9 (NRSV)

[Father Evagrius continued,] "But keep the day of resurrection and of presentation to God in remembrance also. Imagine the fearful and terrible judgment. Consider the fate kept for sinners, their shame before the face of God and the angels and archangels and all men. . . . Consider also the good things in store for the righteous: confidence in the face of God the Father and his Son, the angels and archangels and all the people of the saints, the kingdom of heaven, and the gifts of that realm, joy and beatitude. Remember well these two realities. Weep for the judgment of sinners. . . . But rejoice and be glad at the lot of the righteous. Strive to obtain those joys, but be a stranger to those pains. Whether you are inside or outside your prayer chamber, be careful that you never forget these things, so that you may at least flee wrong and harmful thoughts."
—*The Wisdom of the Desert Fathers and Mothers*

I will live for You today because I know that I am living for eternity.

July

═══ JULY 1 ═══

*C*onsider it a sheer gift, friends, when tests and challenges come at you from all sides. You know that under pressure, your faith-life is forced into the open and shows its true colors. So don't try to get out of anything prematurely. Let it do its work so you become mature and well-developed, not deficient in any way.

—James 1:2–4 (THE MESSAGE)

"We must shun such phrases as: 'I had right on my side'; 'They had no right to do this to me'; 'The person who treated me like this was not right.' May God deliver us from such a false idea of right. Do you think it was right that our good Jesus had to endure so many insults? Were those who hurled insults at Him right, and did they have the right to do those wrongs to Him? I do not know why anyone is in a convent if she is willing to bear only those crosses she thinks she has a right to expect."

—St. Teresa of Avila

Whatever I have to endure, Lord, I can, and I will.

═══ JULY 2 ═══

[*I*]f my people who are called by my name humble themselves, pray, seek my face, and turn from their wicked ways, then I will hear from heaven, and will forgive their sin and heal their land. —2 Chronicles 7:14 (NRSV)

"God keep us from being like that [worrying about our 'rights']. Let the sister who thinks she is the least among others consider herself the happiest and most fortunate. If she lives her life as she should, she will, as a rule, lack no honor either in this life or in the next. Let us, my daughters, imitate the great humility of the most sacred Virgin, whose habit we wear and whose nuns we are unashamed to call ourselves. Let us imitate this humility in some degree, because no matter how much we humble ourselves, we fall short of being the daughters of such a Mother and the brides of such a Spouse." —St. Teresa of Avila

It is an honor to have little in the world, for the sake of You.

=== JULY 3 ===

$\mathcal{G}$od abides in those who confess that Jesus is the Son
of God, and they abide in God. So we have known
and believe the love that God has for us.
—1 John 4:15–16 (NRSV)

"Faith tells us of things we have never seen or understood. We have never seen or understood anything that resembles them, since there is nothing that resembles them at all. We have no light of natural knowledge about them, since what we are told about these things bears no relation to any of our senses. We know it by the ear alone, believing what we are taught, bringing our natural light into subjection, and treating it as if it did not exist." —St. John of the Cross

Bless me with faith and hope, today, O Lord.

═══ JULY 4 ═══

*There is no fear in love. But perfect love drives out fear,
because fear has to do with punishment. The one who
fears is not made perfect in love.*
—1 John 4:18 (NIV)

God explained to St. Catherine of Siena: "The eye of holy faith
looks not only at the punishment of sin, but at the fruit of virtue,
and the love that I bear to the soul, so that it may climb with love
and affection and be stripped of servile fear. And doing so, such
souls will become faithful and not unfaithful servants, serving
Me through love and not through fear."

I will serve You today in love, without fear.

═══ JULY 5 ═══

*"O my dove, in the clefts of the rock, in the covert of the cliff,
let me see your face, let me hear your voice; for your voice is
sweet, and your face is lovely."* —Song of Songs 2:14 (NRSV)

"God . . .want[s] to call to Himself the littlest and weakest of all.
He . . . is pleased to show His goodness and His power by using
the least worthy instruments. But Jesus knew how weak I was,
and it was for that reason that He hid me first in the cleft in the
rock." —St. Thérèse of Lisieux

Thank You for hiding me when I need Your nurture and protection.

*F*or what will it profit a man if he gains the whole
world and forfeits his soul? Or what shall a man
give in return for his soul?
—Matthew 16:26 (ESV)

"About everything St. Francis did there was something that was in a good sense childish, and even in a good sense willful. He threw himself into things abruptly, as if they had just occurred to him. . . . He never thought of waiting for introductions or bargains or any of the considerable backing that he already had from rich and responsible people. He simply saw a boat and threw himself into it." —G. K. Chesterton

**I will no longer use the excuse of unpreparedness
to do Your work.**

=== JULY 7 ===

"*B*ehold, I am coming soon. . . . I am the Alpha and the
Omega, the first and the last, the beginning and the end."
Blessed are those who wash their robes, so that they
may have the right to the tree of life and that they
may enter the city by the gates.
—Revelation 22:12–14 (ESV)

"When Father Agathon sailed in a boat, he was the first to handle the oars. When the brothers came to see him, he set the table

with his own hands, as soon as they had prayed, because he was full of God's love. When he was at the point of death, he remained three days with his eyes fixed, wide-open. The brothers roused him, saying, 'Father, where are you?' He replied, 'I am standing before the judgment seat of God.' They said, 'Aren't you afraid?' He replied, 'Until this moment, I have done my best to keep God's commandments; but I am a man; how should I know if my deeds are acceptable to God?' The brothers said to him, 'Don't you have confidence that you have lived your life according to the God's law?' The old man replied, 'I won't have any confidence until I meet God. Truly God's judgment is not human judgment.' When they wanted to question him further, he said to them, 'Don't talk to me anymore . . . I no longer have time.' So he died with joy. They saw him depart like one greeting his dearest friends. He preserved the strictest watchfulness in all things, saying, 'Without great watchfulness a person does not advance in even a single virtue.'"
—*The Wisdom of the Desert Fathers and Mothers*

Wake me up, today, O Christ. Every moment is precious.

═══ JULY 8 ═══

[*Jesus*, said,] "You shall love the Lord your God with all your heart, and with all your soul, and with all your mind. This is the greatest and first commandment. And a second is like it: You shall love your neighbor as yourself.

—Matthew 22:37–39 (NRSV)

"Do you see how Jesus clearly intimates that love is greater than martyrdom? For if a father had a beloved child on whose behalf he would even give up his life, but if someone were to love the father and completely ignore the son, he would infuriate the father. He wouldn't experience any love himself because of the overlooking of his son. Now, if this could happen with a father and a son, how much more with God and each of us? Since surely God is more loving than any parent." —St. John Chrysostom

Show me how to love You more.

═══ JULY 9 ═══

I, I am he who blots out your transgressions for my own sake,
and I will not remember your sins.
—Isaiah 43:25 (NRSV)

St. Teresa of Avila confesses to her readers: "I am greatly confused about urging this virtue upon you, for I ought to have practiced a little bit of what I am recommending to you. I confess, though, that I have made very little progress. I always seem to be able to find a reason for thinking I am being virtuous when I make excuses for myself. There are times when this might be lawful, and when not to do it would be wrong, but I don't have the discretion or humility to do it only when it is appropriate. It takes great humility to remain silent when you find yourself unjustly condemned. To do so would be to imitate our Lord, who sets us free from all our sins. Try earnestly to act this way, for it brings great gain. I can see no gain in trying to free ourselves from blame except in those very few cases where hiding the truth might be offensive or cause a scandal."

Lord, show me the sin in my life today.

═ JULY 10 ═

𝒯urn back to the Lord and forsake your sins; pray in his
presence and lessen your offense.
—Sirach 17:25 (NRSV)

Father Evagrius once said, "Take away temptations, and no one
will be saved." —*The Wisdom of the Desert Fathers and Mothers*

**I'm thankful for the temptations that come my way.
They make me stronger.**

═ JULY 11 ═

𝒥'm feeling terrible—I couldn't feel worse! Get me on my
feet again. You promised, remember? When I told my story,
you responded; train me well in your deep wisdom. Help me
understand these things inside and out so I can ponder your
miracle-wonders. My sad life's dilapidated, a falling-down
barn; build me up again by your Word. Barricade the road that
goes Nowhere; grace me with your clear revelation.
—Psalm 119:25–29 (THE MESSAGE)

"For those who desire eternal life, a pure love, detached from themselves, is necessary. For to gain eternal life it is not enough to flee from sin for fear of punishment, or to embrace virtue from the motive of one's own advantage. Sin should be abandoned because it is displeasing to Me, and virtue should be loved for My sake." —St. Catherine of Siena, recording the words of God given to her in a vision

Set me free, Father. Give me wisdom, Holy Spirit.

=== JULY 12 ===

If then you have been raised with Christ,
seek the things that are above.
—Colossians 3:1a (ESV)

"I pray then that we should use every effort to press on toward this life's goal. Let no one look behind him as did Lot's wife, especially since the Lord has said that no one who puts his hand upon the plough and looks back is fit for the kingdom of heaven. To look back means to have second thoughts about your undertaking and to become entangled once more in worldly desires. Do not fear the word 'virtue' as if it were unattainable. Do not think that such an endeavor, which depends on our will, is alien to you or something remote." —St. Antony, as told by St. Athanasius [continued tomorrow . . .]

Make me strong for You, today, Lord.

JULY 13

$\mathcal{D}$on't you know that you yourselves are God's temple and
that God's Spirit dwells in your midst?
—1 Corinthians 3:16 (NIV)

[St. Antony continued,] "We all have a natural inclination to
[seek virtue], and it is something that awaits only our willing-
ness. Let the Greeks pursue their studies across the seas and go
in search of teachers of useless literature in foreign lands. We,
however, feel no compulsion to travel across the waves, for the
kingdom of heaven is to be found everywhere on earth. That is
why the Lord says in the Gospel: 'The kingdom of God is among
you' (Lk. 17:21). The virtue that is within us requires only the
human will." —as told by St. Athanasius

I set my vision, and my will, upon serving You, today.

JULY 14

$\mathcal{F}$or our sake he made him to be sin who did not know sin, so
that we might become the righteousness of God in him.
—2 Corinthians 5:21 (NAB)

"One Sunday, as I was looking at a photograph showing Our
Lord on the Cross, I was struck by the blood that was falling
from one of His Divine hands. I felt great pain at the thought that
this blood was falling to the ground without anyone hurrying to
collect it, and I resolved to keep myself in spirit at the foot of the

Cross in order to receive the Divine dew that was flowing down from it, understanding that I must then spread it over souls, Jesus' cry on the Cross also resounded continually in my heart: 'I am thirsty!' These words set on fire within me a keen fervor that I hadn't known before. I wanted to give something to drink to my Beloved, and I felt myself consumed with thirst for souls."
—St. Thérèse of Lisieux

Show me today where I am supposed to spread Your love.

═══ JULY 15 ═══

[*W*]e are ambassadors for Christ.
—2 Corinthians 5:20a (NAB)

"Oh, my Lord! When I think of the many ways You suffered, many of them undeservedly, I do not know what to say for myself. I don't know what I must have been thinking when I wished for no suffering or what I am doing when I make excuses for myself. For what is it to you, Lord, to give much rather than little? I do not deserve it, but I have not deserved the favors You have already shown me. How can it be that I should want others to think well of someone so evil as me, when they have said such wicked things about You, who are good above all other good? It is intolerable, my God. I do not want You to have to tolerate in me anything that is displeasing in Your eyes. Give me light and make me want fervently that all should hate me, since I have often left You, who have loved me so faithfully." —St. Teresa of Avila

You saved me. What should I do?

[*Jesus*] said, "Abba, Father, for you all things are possible."
—Mark 14:36a (NRSV)

"The image of God as Abba—Father or Daddy—was the fire crackling in the soul of Jesus. Everything that Jesus taught and did radiated from it: His outreach to the marginalized, His table fellowship with sinners, and His parables about love, forgiveness, and generosity were all sparks shooting from His insight that God was an amazingly close and intimate Father."
—Fr. Albert Haase, OFM

**What is my most recurring image of God?
How might that affect my spiritual life?**

== JULY 17 ==

Jesus said, "If? There are no 'ifs' among believers. Anything can happen." No sooner were the words out of his mouth than the father cried, "Then I believe. Help me with my doubts!"
—Mark 9:23–24 (THE MESSAGE)

"Other knowledge can be acquired by the light of the understanding, but the knowledge that comes from faith is acquired without the enlightenment of the understanding, which is rejected for faith. So Isaiah said: 'If you do not believe, you will not understand. It is clear, then, that faith is a dark night for the

soul, and it is in this way that it gives it light. The more the soul is darkened, the greater is the light that comes to it."
—St. John of the Cross

I want to believe. Help me with my doubts.

═══ JULY 18 ═══

*G*od indeed is my salvation; I am confident and unafraid.
—Isaiah 12:2a (NAB)

"In the beginning, a person serves Me imperfectly through servile fear. But by practice and perseverance, he or she arrives at the love of delight, finding delight and profit in Me. This is a necessary stage through which he or she must pass in order to attain perfect love. I call filial love perfect, because by it, a person receives inheritance from Me, the eternal Father, and because a child's love includes that of a friend, which is why I told you that a friend grows into a child."
—St. Catherine of Siena, listening to God speak to her soul

I come to You today with simple love, not fear.

$\mathscr{S}$ing a new song to the LORD, for he has done marvelous deeds.
—Psalm 98:1a (NAB)

"Reading . . . can be prayer. Christianity, of course, is not a 'religion of the book' but rather faith in the Word—in that Word of God who in Mary's womb 'was made flesh' and 'lived among us, and we saw his glory.' . . . Books have a spiritual function. . . . [P]rayerful reading, known as *lectio divina*, in fact opens the reader to Christ and implies a capacity to understand that only God can give. St. Irenaeus, recalling the time that Moses spent on Sinai in direct contact with the Most High, affirmed that 'in those forty days he learned how to remember God's words, His characteristic style, the spiritual images He employed and His way of prefiguring future events.'" —Timothy Verdon

I will read the Holy Scriptures, spending time with the Word, today.

=== JULY 20 ===

$\mathscr{I}$f you don't know what you're doing, pray to the Father. He loves to help. You'll get his help, and won't be condescended to when you ask for it. Ask boldly, believingly, without a second thought. People who "worry their prayers" are like wind-whipped waves. Don't think you're going to get anything from the Master that way, adrift at sea, keeping all your options open.
—James 1:5–8 (THE MESSAGE)

"For now, oh my God, it is to You alone that I can talk, because nobody else will understand. . . . I hear You saying to me . . . 'I will give you what you desire. . . . I will lead you by the way that you cannot possibly understand.'" —Thomas Merton OCSO

There are so many things I don't understand, Lord.

JULY 21

*P*ersevere . . . being watchful . . .
making the most of the opportunity.
—Colossians 4:2–5 (NAB)

"Mother Theodora was one of the great women ascetics of the desert. . . . She once asked Archbishop Theophilus about some words of the Apostle, saying, 'What does this mean, making the most of the opportunity?' He said to her, 'This saying shows us how to profit at all times. For example, is it a time of excess for you? Through humility and patience buy up the time of excess, and draw profit from it. Is it a time of shame? Buy it up by means of resignation and win it. So everything that goes against us can, if we wish, become profitable to us. Mother Theodora said, 'Let us strive to enter by the narrow gate. Just as the trees, if they have not stood before the winter's storms, cannot bear fruit, so it is with us. This present age is a storm, and it is only through many trials and temptations that we can obtain an inheritance in the kingdom of heaven.'"
—*The Wisdom of the Desert Fathers and Mothers*

What fruit am I bearing, today?

*N*ear indeed is [God's] salvation for those who fear him;
glory will dwell in our land. Love and truth will meet;
justice and peace will kiss.
—Psalm 85:10–11 (NAB)

St. Teresa of Avila was writing for her fellow nuns, but the lesson is important for all: "Do not suppose that either the evil or the good you do will remain secret, no matter how strictly you are enclosed. Do you think, daughters, that if you do not make excuses for yourself there will not be someone else who will defend you? Remember how the Lord took St. Mary Magdalene's part in the Pharisee's house and also when her sister blamed her. He will not treat you as rigorously as he treated Himself. It was not until He was on the cross that He had even a thief to defend Him. . . . Be glad when you are blamed, and in time you will see what gains your soul experiences."

I will take no offenses today. I will feel no slights.

*H*ear this . . . you who swear by the name of the LORD and invoke the God of Israel without sincerity, without justice.
—Isaiah 48:1 (NAB)

"My desire to save souls has been growing every day. It seems to me that I can hear Jesus tell me, as He did to the Samaritan woman, 'Give me a drink!' [cf. John 4:6–15]. This was a true exchange of love: To souls I gave the blood of Jesus; to Jesus I offered these same souls, refreshed by His divine dew. In that way it seemed to me that I was quenching His thirst."

—St. Thérèse of Lisieux

What can I do to save a soul today, Lord?

═══ **JULY 24** ═══

"All Saints Convent"
by Bonnie Thurston

In an indifferent world,
Detached from the sands of time,
Your house stands on a rock
And gathers the faceless ones
Around a table
Where the undeserving
Are honored guests.

We come from darkness,
Bring our hungers and thirsts.
We join you, kneel at dawn
Under a single, amber light,
No more strangers,
But sisters in the Silence
Who speaks us all.

I want to be in the blessed company of Your saints.

If only you would attend to my commandments,
your peace would be like a river.
—Isaiah 48:18 (NAB)

Christ speaking to St. Catherine of Siena: "You cannot repay the love that I require of you. Therefore I have placed you in the midst of your brothers and sisters, so that you may do to them that which you cannot do to Me. That is, I give you the opportunity to love your neighbor of free grace, without expecting any return. What you do to him, I count as done to Me.

Who is my neighbor, today?

Don't love the world's ways. Don't love the world's goods.
Love of the world squeezes out love for the Father. Practically
everything that goes on in the world—wanting your own way,
wanting everything for yourself, wanting to appear important—
has nothing to do with the Father. It just isolates you from him.
The world and all its wanting, wanting, wanting is on the way
out—but whoever does what God wants is set for eternity.
—1 John 2:15–17 (The Message)

"The young musician from Ohio was mesmerized by New York City and very excited about her upcoming audition. As she emerged from the subway at the corner of 56th and Seventh, however, she felt disoriented. She knew her destination was around here somewhere, but in which direction. Then, to her relief, she saw an elderly man coming toward her, with a violin case tucked under his arm. Ah, he must surely know, so she inquired, 'Excuse me sir, can you tell me how to get to Carnegie Hall?' The old musician halted, looked pensive for a moment, and then offered, 'Practice, practice, practice.' We can say the same about Catholic Christian faith; to be any good at it, requires lots of practice." —Thomas Groome

Am I practicing my faith as much as I should?

═ JULY 27 ═

When I was a boy at my father's knee, the pride and joy of my mother, he would sit me down and drill me: "Take this to heart. Do what I tell you—live! Sell everything and buy Wisdom! Forage for Understanding! Don't forget one word! Don't deviate an inch!"
—Proverbs 4:3–5 (THE MESSAGE)

"'We are not born Christians, we become Christians' (Tertullian). This 'becoming' is the space in which Christian asceticism reveals its meaning. The word *asceticism* is suspect today, if not completely absurd and incomprehensible for many people, including—and this is particularly significant—quite a few Christians. Derived from the Greek verb *askein* (to train or practice), the term indicates a form of methodical training, a repeated exercise, an effort directed toward the acquisition of a specific ability or area of competence. We might think of an athlete, an artist, or a soldier—each trains by repeating over and over the same movements or gestures in order to reach a high level of performance. Asceticism, therefore, is first of all a human necessity." —Enzo Bianchi

**Lent is long past, but every day is an opportunity
to make more room in my life for You.**

=== JULY 28 ===

The ways of right-living people glow with light;
the longer they live, the brighter they shine. But the
road of wrongdoing gets darker and darker—travelers
can't see a thing; they fall flat on their faces.
—Proverbs 4:18–19 (THE MESSAGE)

"I trust the Lord to help me say a few words that will assist those who have set out on the road of virtue but make no progress as they pass through the dark night to divine union. Sometimes they have no desire to enter this journey; at other times they do not have competent spiritual advisers to guide them. It is sad to see so many souls to whom God gives both aptitude and favor with which to make progress, remaining in an elementary stage of communion with God for lack of will or knowledge, or because there is no one who will lead them in the right path or teach them how to go beyond the beginnings." —St. John of the Cross

Teach me, Lord, to go beyond.

JULY 29

I praise you, LORD, for you raised me up.
—Psalm 30:2a (NAB)

"Even if the whole world blames you, what does it matter as long as you are in God's arms? He is powerful enough to free you from everything; only once did He command the world to be made and it was done. With Him, to will is to do. Do not be afraid if He takes pleasure in speaking to you. He does this for the greater good of those who love Him. His love for those who hold Him dear is not weak; He shows us in every possible way. Why, then, do we not show Him our highest love?" —St. Teresa of Avila

**I will spend a few minutes just resting in God's arms.
I will let everything else go.**

JULY 30

I believe I shall see the LORD's goodness
in the land of the living.
—Psalm 27:13 (NAB)

"In a short time God had managed to pull me out of the narrow circle in which I was spinning without knowing how to get out. When I see the road that He had me travel, my gratitude is great. But I must admit that if the biggest step was taken, I still had many things to get rid of." —St. Thérèse of Lisieux

What do I need to get rid of?

I urge you . . . to offer your bodies as a living sacrifice, holy and pleasing to God. . . .
—Romans 12:1 (NAB)

"The more emphasis the soul lays on what it understands, experiences, and imagines, and the more it esteems this, the more it loses of the supreme good, and the more it is hindered from attaining the supreme good. The less it thinks of what it may have and the more it dwells on the highest good, the closer it will get to this higher good." —St. John of the Cross

Show me what's really good, Lord.

August

*D*o you conform yourselves to this age but be transformed
by the renewal of your mind, that you may discern what
is the will of God, what is good and pleasing and perfect.
—Romans 12:2 (NAB)

"If your neighborly love is still imperfect, this is because,
although your love was originally drawn from Me, the fountain
of all love, you took the vessel out of the water in order to drink
from it. Your love for Me is still imperfect, and your neighborly
love is so weak, because the root of self-love has not been prop-
erly dug out."
—St. Catherine of Siena, listening to God speaking

May there be less of me and more of You.

"Through and Beyond"
by Bonnie Thurston

One must be faithful
to her own, particular
darkness and doubt,
walk the way of unknowing,
live through and beyond
habituated fears.

The imprisoned imagination
instinctively knows
chains that bind softly
are still chains
and holding self tightly
poisons the heart.

Many thresholds beckon,
some delightful, some devilish.
The door is always open.
One deep, grateful breath,
one small step forward
has power to change everything.

Is there something I need to change?

═══ AUGUST 3 ═══

"Blessed are the meek, for they will inherit the land."
—Matthew 5:5 (NAB)

"The will cannot contain within itself both passion for created things and passion for God. What does the created thing have to do with the Creator? What does the sensual have to do with the spiritual? The visible with the invisible? The temporal with the eternal? Christlike poverty of spirit with attachment to anything in the world?" —St. John of the Cross

I want my passion for You to exceed my passion for other people and things, even though it's hard.

═ AUGUST 4 ═

"*B*lessed are the clean of heart, for they will see God."
—Matthew 5:8 (NAB)

"What it was exactly that happened [on Mount La Verna to St. Francis of Assisi] may never be known. The matter has been, I believe, a subject of dispute among the most devout students of the saintly life as well as between such students and others of the more secular sort. It may be that St. Francis never spoke to a soul on the subject." —G. K. Chesterton

If St. Francis didn't discuss his miracle, I can keep quiet about the blessings You are bestowing on me.

═ AUGUST 5 ═

"*Y*ou are the salt of the earth."
—Matthew 5:13a (NAB)

"God deliver us from saying, 'We are not angels,' or 'We are not saints,' whenever we commit some sin. We may not be. But, what a good thing it is for us to reflect that we can be if we will only try and if God gives us His hand. Do not be afraid that He will fail to do His part if we do not fail to do ours. Do not let there be anything we know of that would serve the Lord and that, with His help, we would not do. We must always have courage, which God gives to the strong. He will give courage to you and to me."
—St. Teresa of Avila

No excuses. I will live for You today.

═══ **AUGUST 6** ═══

$\mathscr{G}$od is love, and those who abide in love abide in
God, and God abides in them.
—1 John 4:16b (NRSV)

"The first and great commandment is, 'You shall love the Lord
your God,' and then He adds the second (never wanting the first
to be heard alone), which is like it: 'You shall love your neighbor
as yourself.' Listen: if this were truly observed there would be
neither slave nor free, neither ruler nor ruled, neither rich nor
poor, neither small nor great. And no devil would ever have to
become known." —St. John Chrysostom

**I will refocus, starting today, on the kind of loving
that takes a lot of work and a lot of time.**

═══ **AUGUST 7** ═══

$\mathscr{B}$ut as it is written, "What no eye has seen, nor ear heard,
nor the human heart conceived, what God has
prepared for those who love him."
—1 Corinthians 2:9 (NRSV)

"All the great truths of religion, the mysteries of eternity, plunged
my soul into a happiness that was not of earth. I was already
feeling what God reserves for those who love Him (not with the
human eye, but with that of the heart), and seeing that eternal
rewards have no proportion to the slight sacrifices of life, I

wanted to love, love Jesus with passion, give Him a thousand signs of love while I could still do it." —St. Thérèse of Lisieux

I want to know You better, Lord.

AUGUST 8

*B*e sober and vigilant. Your opponent the devil
is prowling around like a roaring lion. . . .
—1 Peter 5:8 (NAB)

God once revealed to St. Catherine of Siena these words: "During the time ordained for prayer, the devil is apt to arrive in the soul, causing much more conflict and trouble than when the soul is not occupied in prayer. He does this so that holy prayer may become tedious to the soul. He tempts the soul often with these words: 'This prayer avails you nothing,'"

**Please strengthen me, God, right now! Give me
ten minutes of uninterrupted attention.**

AUGUST 9

*T*he God of all grace who called you to his eternal glory
through Christ [Jesus] will himself restore, confirm,
strengthen, and establish you. . . .
—1 Peter 5:10 (NAB)

"Mother Theodora once said, 'A devout man happened to be insulted by someone, and he said to the person, "I could say as much to you, but God's commandment keeps my mouth shut."'"
—*The Wisdom of the Desert Fathers and Mothers*

Help me, Lord! Help me do what I know I'm supposed to do.

═══ AUGUST 10 ═══

𝒯he root of wisdom—to whom has it been revealed?
Her subtleties—who knows them?
—Sirach 1:6 (NRSV)

"Wisdom is a gift of the heart, centered upon experience, not a collection of concepts learned through books or years of study. It is the beam of light that permeates everything and reveals to us the presence of God in each person, event, and circumstance in life. It is the glow of gentleness in the midst of a harsh world; the glimmer of hope that shines across the dark sky of suffering and pain; the shafts of comfort that come when our life is in disarray. This gift is the radiance that shines through acts of loving forgiveness as we live with the mind of Christ, and the glare of self-knowledge that calls us to personal transformation."
—Sr. Bridget Haase, OSU [continued tomorrow . . .]

Where do I find Wisdom?

*W*isdom teaches her children and gives help to those
who seek her. Whoever loves her loves life.
—Sirach 4:11–12a (NRSV)

[Sr. Bridget Haase, OSU, continues,] "Wisdom is the north star
of our journey that shows us the path to walk and lets us know
where we are headed. It is the illumination of experiencing
within our being, and not merely in our heads, that 'no eye has
seen, nor ear heard, nor the human heart conceived, what God
has prepared for those who love him.' (1 Cor. 2:9) As we anticipate the refulgence of what is yet to come, can we be wise and
stand in awe under the night sky and bask in the glow of the
twinkling stars?"

**When I try and comprehend You, God, I'm baffled.
I'm struck silent.**

"*B*lessed are they who mourn, for they will be comforted."
—Matthew 5:4 (NAB)

"Humility is the principal virtue that people who pray must
practice. It is important that you should try to learn how to practice it often. How can anyone who is truly humble think she is
as good as those who become contemplatives? Of course, in His
goodness and mercy God can make her a contemplative. But my

advice is that she should always sit in the lowest place, for that is what the Lord taught us to do by both His words and deeds. Let her prepare herself to let God lead her down this road if He so wills it. If not, she should consider herself happy in serving God's servants and in praising Him." —St. Teresa of Avila

It is okay for me to feel "low," and to stay there, with God.

═ AUGUST 13 ═

So here's what I want you to do, God helping you:
Take your everyday, ordinary life—your sleeping, eating,
going-to-work, and walking-around life—and place it before
God as an offering.
—Romans 12:1 (THE MESSAGE)

"Union of the soul with God is attained when the likeness that comes from love is produced. We will therefore call this the union of likeness, even as that other union is called substantial or essential. The former is natural, the latter supernatural. The latter happens when the two wills—that of the soul and that of God—are conformed together in one, and there is nothing in the one that repels the other. When the soul rids itself totally of what is repelled by the divine will, refusing to conform to it, it is transformed in God through love." —St. John of the Cross

Transform me today, Christ. Make me more like You.

AUGUST 14

We don't yet see things clearly. We're squinting in a fog, peering through a mist. But it won't be long before the weather clears and the sun shines bright! We'll see it all then, see it all as clearly as God sees us, knowing him directly just as he knows us!
—1 Corinthians 13:12 (THE MESSAGE)

"As the *Imitation of Christ* says, God sometimes communicates Himself amidst great splendor, and sometimes 'gently veiled, in the form of shadows and figures.' It was in this manner that He deigned to manifest Himself to our souls."
—St. Thérèse of Lisieux

Help me see You in the shadows.

AUGUST 15

To you we owe our hymn of praise, O God on Zion.
—Psalm 65:2a (NAB)

God said to St. Catherine of Siena: "The soul should not say its vocal prayers without joining them to mental prayer. That is, while you are reciting vocal prayers, you should endeavor to elevate your mind in My love."

You are in my heart and mind. I'm not only praying; I'm listening.

"Elegy"
by Br. Paul Quenon, OCSO

Bell strokes telling time,
casually fall over retaining wall,
and lazily spill through the valley
entangled in their echoes.

Low sun stretched aslant
long shadows on November grass
empty staff lines of some melody,
never sung,
waiting for its notes.

None will come now.

A life has passed that made
notes enough for seasons full–
and then some.

This empty time stands quieted of
sounds departed.

Yet lingers still a subtle tangle,
an echo come
from what immortal hills?

Who am I remembering today?

AUGUST 17

$\mathcal{F}$or our struggle is not against enemies of blood and flesh,
but against the rulers, against the authorities, against the
cosmic powers of this present darkness, against the spiritual
forces of evil in the heavenly places.
—Ephesians 6:12 (NRSV)

"We ought to be careful to ensure that we control the tyrannical passion of anger, since it says in the Bible, 'your anger does not produce God's righteousness' (Jas. 1:20), and 'Desire gives birth to sin, and that sin, when fully grown, gives birth to death' (Jas. 1:15). The divine voice has recommended that we should protect our soul with unceasing vigilance and lead it toward perfection with all care and effort, because we have enemies who are trained to trip us up. These are the demons whom we must fight without a truce." —St. Antony, as relayed by St. Athanasius

Spirit of God, I will focus on my unresolved anger today.

AUGUST 18

$\mathcal{O}$ God, you are my God—it is you I seek!
—Psalm 63:2a (NAB)

"God does not lead us all by the same road, and maybe she who believes that she is going by the lowest road is the highest in God's eyes. Thus, it does not follow that just because we all practice prayer, we are all going to become contemplatives [experience union with God]. Those of us who are not contemplatives would be greatly discouraged if we did not understand the truth that contemplation is something given by God. Since it is not necessary for our salvation, God does not give it to us before He gives us our reward. . . . The Lord will be laying up for us all that we cannot enjoy in this life. We should not be discouraged, then, and give up prayer or stop doing what the others are doing. The Lord might give us great rewards all at once as He has been giving to others over many years." —St. Teresa of Avila [continued tomorrow . . .]

I will pray today even if it means walking or sitting quietly, saying nothing.

═ AUGUST 19 ═

$\mathscr{F}$or you my body yearns; for you my soul thirsts, in a land parched, lifeless, and without water.
—Psalm 63:2b (NAB)

[St. Teresa of Avila continues,] "St. Martha was holy, but we are not told that she was a contemplative. What more could you want than to grow to be like her, who was worthy to receive Christ our Lord so often in her house, and to prepare meals for Him, and to serve Him and perhaps eat at table with Him? If she had been always absorbed in devotion, as St. Mary Magdalene was, no one would have prepared a meal for this Divine Guest. . . . Contemplatives know that, although they themselves may be silent, the Lord will speak for them. As a rule, this makes them forget themselves and everything else. Remember that there must be someone to cook the meals. Count yourselves happy in being able to serve like Martha. Remember that true humility consists in being ready for what the Lord wants to do with you and happy that He should do it, and in considering yourselves unworthy to be called His servants."

I am ready to do what You have for me.

=== AUGUST 20 ===

I think of you upon my bed, I remember you
through the watches of the night.
—Psalm 63:7 (NAB)

"But one thing I tell you: He is a jealous lover and permits no other relationships, and He chooses not to work in your will unless He is with you alone by Himself. He asks no help, but only your self. He wills that you both gaze on Him and leave Him alone. And that you keep the windows and the door closed against flies and Enemies attacking. And if you are willing to do this, you must humbly set upon Him with prayer, and soon He will help you." —*The Cloud of Unknowing*

My windows and doors are closed, Lord. I'm alone with You.

AUGUST 21

*M*y Master God showed me this vision: A bowl of fresh
fruit. He said, "What do you see, Amos?" I said,
"A bowl of fresh, ripe fruit."
—Amos 8:1–2a (THE MESSAGE)

"When a gardener pours out attention on a fruit that he wants to
mature before its season, it's never to leave it hanging from the
tree, but in order to serve it on a brilliantly set table. It was with
such an intention that Jesus poured out His graces on [me,] His
little flower." —St. Thérèse of Lisieux

Watch today, Lord, as my faith flowers into fruit.

AUGUST 22

*G*ive liberally and be ungrudging when you do so,
for on this account the LORD your God will bless
you in all your work and in all that you undertake.
—Deuteronomy 15:10 (NRSV)

"Jesus makes it clear that *how* we give is just as important as *what*
we give. Almsgiving is a spontaneous response to a need at hand.
It happens quietly with no thought of how this contribution or
assistance will benefit me, win personal applause, or polish my
reputation in my neighborhood community or parish. Giving
without being noticed is to follow the way of Christ. Our secret
acts of charity and loving sharing strip away our pride, purify

our intentions, and transform a hand-out into a Gospel witness."
—Sr. Bridget Haase, osu

**Lord, put in my path opportunities to give.
Open my eyes to see them.**

=== AUGUST 23 ===

I will bless you as long as I live; I will lift up my hands,
calling on your name.
—Psalm 63:5 (NAB)

St. Catherine of Siena heard these words of the Lord: "Perfect prayer is not arrived at through many words, but through affection of desire, when the soul raises itself to Me, knowing itself and My mercy, seasoning the one with the other. Thus, the soul will practice mental and vocal prayer together, for even as the active and contemplative life are one, so are they."

I don't have many words today.

=== AUGUST 24 ===

"*The* Great Bell"
by Br. Paul Quenon, ocso

Beneath darkened eaves
all busy with twitter,
swallows anticipate

light enough to fly,
quite beside themselves with
excitement 'til the great

bell's torque, rock and iron clang,
imperiously rounded
the cloister court which trapped,

turned and intensified
sound up the late chilled night
where angels distracted

with timeless things were rung
down to join monks and swallows
in the timely work of

inviting in the dawn.

Thank You for this new day.

AUGUST 25

[Jesus said,] "The world is full of so-called prayer warriors who are prayer-ignorant. They're full of formulas and programs and advice, peddling techniques for getting what you want from God. Don't fall for that nonsense. This is your Father you are dealing with, and he knows better than you what you need. With a God like this loving you, you can pray very simply. Like this: Our Father in heaven. . . ."
—Matthew 6:7–9a (THE MESSAGE)

"It is always a great thing to base your prayer on prayers that the Lord spoke with His own lips. People are quite right to say this. If our own devotion weren't so weak, we would not need any other systems of prayer or books. I am speaking to those who are unable to recollect themselves by meditating on the mysteries and who think they need special methods of prayer. Some people have such an ingenious mind that nothing is good enough for them." —St. Teresa of Avila

I will take a few minutes, twice today, to pray the Our Father and the Rosary.

$=$ AUGUST 26 $=$

$\mathcal{D}$ear in the eyes of the Lord is the death of his devoted.
—Psalm 116:15 (NAB)

"Would that we could take lessons in what to expect and how it feels to die or what it is like to see the face of the God we have tried to love for a lifetime. But death will always be God's best-kept secret and remains our test. Dying is like those first steps we took as a child after our mother let go and our father extended waiting arms, or that game of blindfolded trust walks we enjoyed in summer camp, or perhaps even the times we were encouraged to fall backward in another's outstretched arms. In each instance all we could do was to trust the one who promised to reach for us, guide us, or catch us." —Sr. Bridget Haase, OSU

Most Sacred Heart of Jesus, I accept whatever You have for me.

"*F*or the gate is narrow and the road is hard that
leads to life, and there are few who find it."
—Matthew 7:14 (NRSV)

"How narrow is the gate and how narrow the way that leads unto
life, and few there are that find it! It is as if Our Savior had said:
In truth the way is narrow, more so than you think. We must
note that He says first that the gate is narrow, to make it clear
that in order for the soul to enter by this gate, which is Christ,
and which comes at the beginning of the road, the will must first
be narrowed and detached from all things sensual and temporal,
and it must love God above them all." —St. John of the Cross

Point me, Holy Spirit, to that narrow portal.

══ **AUGUST 28** ══

I kept faith, even when I said, "I am greatly afflicted!"
—Psalm 116:10 (NAB)

"I was to pass through many trials, but the Divine call was so
pressing that even if I had had to pass through flames, I would
have done so in order to be faithful to Jesus."
—St. Thérèse of Lisieux

**What trials am I facing right now? I will bring
them to God in prayer.**

AUGUST 29

*L*ive by the Spirit.
—Galatians 5:16a (NRSV)

God spoke thus to St. Catherine of Siena: "I have told you that a holy desire is a continual prayer."

**May this be true in my life today, Lord: may
I carry holy desire for only You.**

AUGUST 30

"*L*et me give you a new command: Love one another. In the same way I loved you, you love one another. This is how everyone will recognize that you are my disciples—when they see the love you have for each other."
—John 13:34–35 (THE MESSAGE)

"The daily practice of Christian faith . . . cannot be reduced to saying prayers or doing spiritual exercises. The core Christian practices are to live the great commandment of love, to embrace the spirit of the Beatitudes, to do the works of mercy and compassion, to work for justice and peace in the world. In sum, our practice of Christian faith should help to realize the reign of God. We cannot simply pray for its coming, as in 'thy kingdom come'; we must also do God's will 'on earth,' i.e. in daily life, 'as it is done in heaven.' This is what it means to live as a disciple of Jesus." —Thomas Groome [continued tomorrow . . .]

Thy will be done, Lord. Tell me: what can I do?

AUGUST 31

*Justice will march before him, and make
a way for his footsteps.*
—Psalm 85:14 (NAB)

[Thomas Groome continues,] "[An] emphasis on practicing the faith, living as disciples, lends a particular distinction to Catholic spirituality. Far more than simply saying prayers or doing pious things, Catholic spirituality requires people to consciously put their faith to work in the ordinary and everyday of life. Catholic spirituality means that Christian faith should permeate and direct our every 'thought, word and deed'—as the old Morning Offering put it. This being said—that Christians are to live their faith through their whole way of being in the world—we then recognize that good habits of prayer and spiritual practices can help to inspire, guide, and sustain such lived faith in the day to day."

*God, the all-powerful Father of our Lord Jesus Christ
has given us a new birth by water and the Holy Spirit,
and forgiven all our sins. May He also keep us faithful
to our Lord Jesus Christ for ever and ever. Amen.*

—from the Renewal of Baptismal Promises

September

SEPTEMBER 1

$\mathcal{Y}$ou are my God; be gracious to me, Lord;
to you I call all the day.
—Psalm 86:2b–3 (NAB)

St. Teresa of Avila believed that the Our Father contained essentially all that we ever needed for prayer. She wrote: "Sometimes when we are most anxious to nurture our devotion, consulting many books will kill it. When a teacher is giving a lesson, she treats her student kindly, hoping the student likes learning, and doing everything she can to help her student learn. The heavenly Teacher treats us in just this way."

Our Father, who art in heaven. . . .

SEPTEMBER 2

$\mathcal{B}$ecause of you friend and neighbor shun me;
my only friend is darkness.
—Psalm 88:19 (NAB)

"Mother Theodora once said that a teacher ought to be a stranger to the desire for domination, vanity, and pride. One should not be able to fool him by flattery, nor blind him by gifts, nor conquer him by the stomach, nor dominate him by anger. But he should be patient, gentle, and humble as far as possible. He must be tested and, without showing favoritism, full of concern, and a lover of souls." —*The Wisdom of the Desert Fathers and Mothers*

Am I being "fooled by flattery," Father, from serving You truly?

SEPTEMBER 3

*Y*ou have turned my mourning into dancing; you have
taken off my sackcloth and clothed me with joy,
so that my soul may praise you and not be silent.
O LORD my God, I will give thanks to you forever.
—Psalm 30:11–12 (NRSV)

"All I have needed Thy hand hath provided. Great is Thy faithfulness, Lord, unto me!" —Thomas Chisholm

My heart is full of praise!

SEPTEMBER 4

I will sing of your mercy forever, LORD.
—Psalm 89:2a (NAB)

"After he had taken farewell of some of his nearest and especially some of his oldest friends, he was lifted at his own request off his own rude bed and laid on the bare ground; as some say clad only in a hair-shirt, as he had first gone forth into the wintry woods from the presence of his father. It was the final assertion of his great fixed idea; of praise and thanks springing to their most towering height out of nakedness and nothing."
—G. K. Chesterton, writing about St. Francis of Assisi

I am conscious that I will die someday, Lord.
Remind me today to focus more intently on You.

SEPTEMBER 5

*W*e love because he first loved us.
—1 John 4:19 (NRSV)

"Love is stronger than any wall, and is firmer than any rock. If you can name any material stronger than walls and rocks, the firmness of love transcends them all. Neither wealth nor poverty overcomes love. The truth is, there would be no poverty, no unbounded wealth, if there were love (cf. Matt. 6:31–34). There would only be the virtuous qualities, without the bad, that stem from each state, poverty and wealth. We would only reap the abundance from wealth, and from poverty we would only have its freedom from care; no one would have to undergo the anxieties of riches or the dread of poverty." —St. John Chrysostom

Christ, show me how to be more gracious to others.

SEPTEMBER 6

*W*hy did I not listen to the voice of my teachers,
incline my ear to my instructors!
—Proverbs 5:13 (NAB)

"I sent the light of the Holy Scriptures to illuminate your blind and coarse understanding, and to lift up the eye of your intellect to know the truth. I, Fire, Acceptor of Sacrifices, ravish away all darkness from you, giving you this light. . . . [N]ot a natural light, but a supernatural one, so that, though in darkness, you might know the truth." —St. Catherine of Siena, listening to God speak.

I want to learn.

═══ SEPTEMBER 7 ═══

$\mathcal{I}$ will give thanks to the LORD with all my heart;
  I will tell of all your wonderful deeds.
          —Psalm 9:1 (NRSV)

"Gratitude involves a conscious choice. I can choose to be grateful even when my emotions and feelings are still steeped in hurt and resentment. I can choose to be grateful when I am criticized, even when my heart still responds in bitterness."
—Henri J. M. Nouwen

My heart is filled with gratitude.

═══ SEPTEMBER 8 ═══

[W]hoever says he abides in him ought to walk
  in the same way in which he walked.
          —1 John 2:6 (ESV)

"Believe only those who model their lives on Christ's life. Strive always to have a good conscience. Practice humility. Despise all worldly things. Believe firmly in the teaching of our Holy Mother

Church. You may then be quite sure you are on a very good road. Stop being afraid of things of which there is no fear. If anyone tries to frighten you, point out the truth in all humility."
—St. Teresa of Avila

I will keep close to You, Christ, and to Your Church.

SEPTEMBER 9

[Jesus said,] "Do not rejoice because the spirits are subject to you, but rejoice because your names are written in heaven."
—Luke 10:20 (NAB)

"I also advise you, my dearest friends, to be more concerned about your way of life than about miracles. If any of you performs miracles, he must neither swell with pride nor look down on those who cannot manage to perform them. Think about each individual's behavior. In this life it is proper for you to imitate what is perfect and to supply what is lacking. It is not for our humble selves to perform miracles but for the power of the Lord." —St. Antony, as told by St. Athanasius

I want to be faithful, Lord, not superhuman.

SEPTEMBER 10

$\mathcal{I}$ am helped, so my heart rejoices; with my song I praise him.
—Psalm 28:7b (NAB)

"When the soul gives itself to prayer it is now like one to whom water has been brought, so that he drinks peacefully, without labor, and is no longer forced to draw the water through the aqueducts of past meditations and forms and figures. Then, as soon as the soul comes before God, it makes an act of knowledge, loving, passive, and tranquil, in which it drinks of wisdom and love and delight." —St. John of the Cross

**Thank You for quenching my spiritual thirst.
You are more than enough.**

SEPTEMBER 11

$\mathcal{M}$y God, my God, why have you forsaken me? Why are you so far from helping me, from the words of my groaning?
—Psalm 22:1 (NRSV)

"I was in a sad desert, or rather my soul was like a fragile skiff with no pilot, at the mercy of the storm-tossed waves. I know, Jesus was there, asleep on my dinghy [cf. Mk. 4:35–41], but the night was so dark that it was impossible for me to see Him. Nothing gave me light; not a single flash of lightning came to pierce the dark clouds." —St. Thérèse of Lisieux [continued tomorrow . . .]

Sometimes I feel lost in the darkness, Lord. Are You still there?

SEPTEMBER 12

O my God, I cry by day, but you do not answer;
and by night, but find no rest.
—Psalm 22:2 (NRSV)

[Continued from yesterday] "Doubtless [when I feel dark and alone], lightning gives off quite a sad glimmer, but at least, if the storm had burst into the open, I would have been able to catch sight of Jesus for an instant. It was night, the deep night of the soul. Like Jesus in the agony in the garden I felt alone, finding comfort neither on earth nor on behalf of heaven. God seemed to have forsaken me!" —St. Thérèse of Lisieux

Even Your disciples felt lost from time to time, Lord.
I know You are there . . . somewhere.

SEPTEMBER 13

I'm speaking to you out of deep gratitude for all that
God has given me, and especially as I have responsibilities in
relation to you. Living then, as every one of you does,
in pure grace, it's important that you not misinterpret
yourselves as people who are bringing this goodness to
God. No, God brings it all to you. The only accurate way to
understand ourselves is by what God is and by what he does
for us, not by what we are and what we do for him.
—Romans 12:3 (THE MESSAGE)

God spoke to St. Catherine of Siena: "You are all trees of love, and without love you cannot live, for you have been made by Me for love. The soul who lives virtuously places the root of its tree in the valley of true humility."

Show me how to become a "tree of love," comfortable in the "valley of humility."

SEPTEMBER 14

Do not worry about anything, but in everything by
prayer and supplication with thanksgiving let your
requests be made known to God.
—Philippians 4:6 (NRSV)

"When we are grateful, we want to share, to reach out, to tell others of the goodness of our benefactor, to bring hope, healing, and happiness to others." —M. Basil Pennington, OCSO

I will share my gratitude with someone today.

SEPTEMBER 15

During the days of Jesus' life on earth, he offered up
prayers and petitions with fervent cries and tears to
the one who could save him from death, and he
was heard because of his reverent submission.
—Hebrews 5:7 (NIV)

"You must know that whether or not you are practicing mental prayer has nothing to do with keeping your lips closed. If, while I am speaking with God, I am fully conscious of doing so, and if this is more real to me than the words I am uttering, then I am combining mental and vocal prayer. I am amazed when people say that they are speaking with God by reciting the Our Father even while they are thinking of worldly things. When you speak with a Lord so great, you should think of who it is you are addressing and what you yourself are, if only that you may speak to Him with proper respect. How can you address a king with the reverence he deserves unless you are clearly conscious of his position and of yours?" —St. Teresa of Avila

I want to keep my mind only on Christ.

=== SEPTEMBER 16 ===

$\mathscr{I}$f I give everything I own to the poor and even go to the stake to be burned as a martyr, but I don't love, I've gotten nowhere. So, no matter what I say, what I believe, and what I do, I'm bankrupt without love.
—1 Corinthians 13:3 (THE MESSAGE)

"[Love] is a choice, a preference. If we love God with our whole hearts, how much heart have we left? If we love with our whole mind and soul and strength, how much mind and soul and strength have we left? We must live this life now. Death changes nothing. If we do not learn to enjoy God now we never will. If we do not learn to praise Him and thank Him and rejoice in Him now, we never will." —Dorothy Day

Please fill me with love, for You are Love.

SEPTEMBER 17

*Keep your heart with all vigilance, for
from it flow the springs of life.*
—Proverbs 4:23 (NRSV)

"Lift up your heart to God. . . . [S]ee to it that you refuse to think on anything but on Himself, so that nothing fills your mind or your will but only Himself. And do all that is in you to forget all the creatures that God ever made and all their works so that neither your thought nor your desire is directed or extended to any of them—neither in general nor in particular. . . . This is the Work of the soul that most pleases God. All the saints and angels take joy in this Work of yours and hasten to further it with all their powers. All the devils are enraged when you do this, and they try as hard as they can to chop your Work down."
—*The Cloud of Unknowing*

Help me focus only on You. Help me put away distractions.

SEPTEMBER 18

And the angel said to me, "Write this: Blessed are those
who are invited to the marriage supper of the Lamb."
And he said to me, "These are true words of God."
—Revelation 19:9 (NRSV)

"Above all, I was growing in the love of God. In my heart I felt
upward impulses that I had not known until then. Sometimes I
was truly transported by love." —St. Thérèse of Lisieux

**I so want to grow in Your love, Lord.
I want deeper connections to You.**

SEPTEMBER 19

O give thanks to the LORD, for he is good; for his
steadfast love endures forever.
—Psalm 107:1 (NRSV)

"Almost the soul's whole work is to realize its unworthiness to
receive such great good and to occupy itself in thanksgiving."
—St. Teresa of Avila

**My days are usually spent proving myself to
people, not to You, God.**

SEPTEMBER 20

𝒜n honest answer is like a warm hug.
First plant your fields; *then* build your barn.
—Proverbs 24:26–27 (The Message)

"You are all trees of love, and without love you cannot live, for you have been made by Me for love. The soul who lives virtuously places the root of its tree in the valley of true humility, but those who live miserably are planted on the mountain of pride."
—St. Catherine of Siena, recalling words God spoke privately to her

I know that true happiness comes from being close to You.

SEPTEMBER 21

[*L*]et us bow down in worship; let us kneel
before the Lord who made us.
—Psalm 95:6 (NAB)

"Although the Rule of St. Benedict was originally addressed to monks, everyone else may benefit from the Holy Patriarch's teaching. He says we should have a reverence for God and also for our neighbor. Reverence is not just interior but is also visible. As novices we were taught how to behave in church: don't just nod your head, make a profound bow. Don't cross your legs.

Don't be looking around. Don't be picking your nose. All of these actions constituted irreverent behavior at prayer."
—Br. Benet Tvedten, OSB

Am I uncomfortable kneeling before God? If so, I will now kneel.

SEPTEMBER 22

*W*hen on his account [of unrighteous people] the earth
was flooded, Wisdom again saved it, piloting
the righteous man on frailest wood.
—Wisdom 10:4 (NAB)

"O You . . . Supreme Goodness, Wisdom Itself, without beginning, without end and without measure in Your works: These are infinite and incomprehensible, a fathomless ocean of wonders, O Beauty containing within yourself all beauties. O Very Strength! O God, help me! I wish I could command all the eloquence of mortals and all wisdom to understand that to know nothing is everything and thus to describe some of the many things on which we may meditate in order to learn something of our Lord's nature." —St. Teresa of Avila

Save me again today, God of Wisdom.

I saw the Lord sitting on a throne, high and lofty; and the hem of his robe filled the temple. Seraphs were in attendance above him; each had six wings: with two they covered their faces, and with two they covered their feet, and with two they flew. And one called to another and said: "Holy, holy, holy is the LORD of hosts; the whole earth is full of his glory."
—Isaiah 6:1–3 (NRSV)

"The Benedictine spirit of reverence toward God finds expression in reverence for everything else: for people, things, and situations. Norvene Vest in her commentary on Chapter 31 of the Rule regarding the office of cellarer, says, 'He is especially to care tenderly for the weak and the vulnerable, whenever possible seeing Christ in those who come to him in need, and treating them as if they themselves—the supplicants—are precious gifts of God, even when their requests are unreasonable.' That is a difficult saying. On the other hand, it's something like my father taught me in the grocery store: the customer isn't always right. But always respect the customer. Benedictine reverence is not confined to bowing profoundly in the presence of God at worship. Its reverence is extended to the people we meet at work and in our homes." —Br. Benet Tvedten, OSB

I am in Your presence. I am awed.
To You all glory and honor, Lord.

God is a safe place to hide, ready to help when we need
him. We stand fearless at the cliff-edge of doom,
courageous in seastorm and earthquake, before the rush
and roar of oceans, the tremors that shift mountains.
Jacob-wrestling God fights for us.
—Psalm 46:1–3a (THE MESSAGE)

"When the spiritual person cannot meditate, let him learn to be
still in God, fixing his loving attention on Him in the calm of his
understanding, although he may think himself to be doing nothing. Little by little, divine calm and peace will be infused into his
soul, together with a wondrous knowledge of God, enfolded in
divine love." —St. John of the Cross

In the quiet, all alone, I am here, Lord.

[Wisdom], when a righteous man fled from his brother's anger,
guided him in right ways, showed him the kingdom of God
and gave him knowledge of holy things.
—Wisdom 10:10a (NAB)

"I know, God doesn't need anyone to do His work, but just as
He allows an able gardener to raise rare and delicate plants, and
for that He gives him the knowledge he needs, but reserves for

Himself the care to make the plants grow—this is how Jesus wants to be helped in his divine cultivation of souls."
—St. Thérèse of Lisieux

How will I be God's "hands" in the world today?

*G*OD spoke all these words: I am GOD, your God, who
brought you out of the land of Egypt, out of a life of
slavery. No other gods, only me.
—Exodus 20:1–3 (THE MESSAGE)

"How we think about God does not come out of nowhere. It is often handed to us by our childhood upbringing, education, and religious formation. A friend of mine Peter who is in his early thirties, still remembers hearing his mother's childhood threat, 'Wait until your father comes home'—and that now raises his blood pressure as he prepares for the Sacrament of Reconciliation. I think I first experienced dread as I hid under the bedcovers the night after stealing a candy bar from a neighbor's kitchen; while a thunderstorm pounded the sky, all I could hear was the priest at the previous Sunday's Mass preaching about God the Father's punishment and wrath." —Fr. Albert Haase, OFM

Do I have an image of God that needs sanctifying?

SEPTEMBER 27

*J*esus answered and said to her, "If you knew the gift of God
and who is saying to you, 'Give me a drink,' you would have
asked him and he would have given you living water."
—John 4:10 (NAB)

"Thanks, thanks be to You, supreme and eternal Father, satisfier
of holy desires, and lover of our salvation, who, through Your
love, gave us Love Himself." —A prayer of St. Catherine of Siena

**I will remember Your love all day, Lord Christ. May
that love fill me today, and help me communicate
Your presence to everyone I meet.**

SEPTEMBER 28

*B*ut you are a chosen race, a royal priesthood, a
holy nation, a people for his own possession, that you
may proclaim the excellencies of him who called you
out of darkness into his marvelous light.
—1 Peter 2:9 (ESV)

"Mother Theodora was asked about the conversations one hears:
'If one is habitually listening to secular speech, how can one yet
live for God alone, as you suggest?' She said, 'Just as when you
are sitting at table and there are many courses, you take some but
without pleasure. So when secular conversations come your way,
have your heart turned toward God. Thanks to this disposition,

you will hear them without pleasure, and they will not do you any harm.'" —*The Wisdom of the Desert Fathers and Mothers*

Help me tune my heart to You today.

═══ SEPTEMBER 29 ═══

$\mathcal{G}$OD's there, listening for all who pray,
for all who pray and mean it.
—Psalm 145:18 (THE MESSAGE)

"Do you think that because we cannot hear God, He is silent? He speaks clearly to the heart when we beg Him from our hearts to do so. It would be a good idea for us to imagine that He has taught this prayer to each one of us individually and that He is continually teaching it to us. The Master is never so far away that the disciple needs to shout to be heard. He is always right at our side. If you want to recite the Our Father well, you must not leave the side of the Master who taught it to you." —St. Teresa of Avila

I know You are beside me.
Our Father. . . .

*J*esus spoke to them again, saying, "I am the light
of the world. Whoever follows me will not
walk in darkness, but will have the light of life."
—John 8:12 (NAB)

"'We began to see Christ in each one that came to us,' Dorothy
Day wrote in describing the early years of the Catholic Worker
Movement. 'If a man came in hungry, there was always something in the icebox. If he needed a bed, and we were crowded,
there was always a bed on the Bowery.' There was always an extra
coat in the closet for someone in need. 'It might be someone
else's coat but that was all right too.'" —Br. Benet Tvedten, OSB

I want to see Your face, Jesus, in those I meet today.

October

═ OCTOBER 1 ═

𝒯oday is the Feast Day of St. Thérèse of Lisieux

"Just as little birds learn to sing by listening to their parents, in the same way children learn the knowledge of virtues, the sublime song of Divine Love, alongside souls that have been charged with forming them in life." —St. Thérèse of Lisieux

**Who has taught me virtue and the love of God?
I will take time to thank them today.**

═ OCTOBER 2 ═

𝒢od-friendship is for God-worshipers; they are
the ones he confides in.
—Psalm 25:14 (THE MESSAGE)

"Since God is vast and boundless, He desires in His prophecies, locutions, and revelations to employ methods of seeing things that differ greatly from such purpose and method as we can normally understand. These are the truer and the more certain, the less they seem so to us. This we constantly see in the Holy Scriptures. To many of the ancients, a number of God's prophecies and locutions did not come to pass as they expected because they understood them after their own manner, in the wrong way, and quite literally." —St. John of the Cross

God, what are You trying to show me today?

OCTOBER 3

On the evening of October 3, 1226, St. Francis of Assisi died.

"Praise to You, O my Lord, for our Sister Death
And the death of the body from whom no one may escape.

Woe to those who die in mortal sin,
But blessed are they who are found walking by Your most holy
    will,
For the second death shall have no power to do them any harm.

Praise to You, O my Lord, and all blessing.
We give You thanks and serve You with great humility."
–St. Francis of Assisi

Dear God, help me live a life that praises You, and help me look forward to death, for I am hungry for heaven.

OCTOBER 4

Today is the Feast Day of St. Francis of Assisi

"I, Brother Francis, a worthless and sinful man, your little servant, bring you greetings in the name of Him who has redeemed and washed us in His precious blood. When you hear His name, adore it with fear and reverence, prostrate on the ground, for He is the Lord Jesus Christ, 'Son of the Most High,' blessed forever!"
—St. Francis of Assisi

What will I do with the one life I have to live?

OCTOBER 5

If I keep my eyes on God, I won't trip over my own feet.
—Psalm 25:15 (The Message)

St. Catherine of Siena heard from God: "Another thing is necessary for you to be pure, and to arrive at union with Me: you should never judge the will of another person in anything that you may see done or said by anyone, either to you or to others. You should consider My will alone, both in them and in yourself. And if you should see evidence of sins or defects, draw the rose out of those thorns. That is, offer them to Me, with holy compassion."

Remind me not to judge anyone, Lord, but to always turn to You with my concerns.

OCTOBER 6

Keep watch over me and keep me out of trouble; don't let me down when I run to you. Use all your skill to put me together; I wait to see your finished product.
—Psalm 25:20–21 (The Message)

St. Teresa of Avila taught her nuns to pray the Our Father and the Hail Mary, saying: "Who could be a better Companion than the Master who taught you the prayer you are about to say? Imagine that this Lord Himself is at your side and look at how lovingly and humbly He teaches you. You should stay with such a good

Friend for as long as you can before you leave Him. If you get used to having Him at your side, and if He sees that you love Him to be there and are always trying to please Him, you will never be able to send Him away and He will never fail you. He will help you in all your trials and you will have Him everywhere. It is a great thing to have such a Friend beside you."

Our Father. . . .

OCTOBER 7

*W*ith my whole heart I cry; answer me, O Lord.
I will keep your statutes.
—Psalm 119:145 (NRSV)

"Antony also used to say that the path to virtue is a wide one if each person were either to watch what he was doing or to report all his thoughts to the brothers. For no one can sin when he has to report all his sins to someone else and endure the shame of revealing his wicked deeds in public. No sinner dares to sin in front of someone else. Even if he does sin, he wants to avoid a witness to his sin and prefers to lie and deny it, thus increasing his error by adding the error of denial." —St. Athanasius

Is it time that I went to Confession?

OCTOBER 8

$\mathcal{Y}$et you are near, O LORD, and all your
commandments are true.
—Psalm 119:151 (NRSV)

"[L]ove may reach to God in this life, but not knowledge. And all the while that the soul dwells in this mortal body, always the sharpness of our understanding in considering all spiritual things—but most especially God—is muddled with a sort of illusion because of which our Work might well be contaminated and it would be a wonder if it did not lead us into great error."
—*The Cloud of Unknowing*

**Bless me in what I don't know, Lord. And bless me
in what I don't need to understand.**

OCTOBER 9

$\mathcal{I}$f I give away all my possessions, and if I hand over my body so that I may boast, but do not have love, I gain nothing.
—1 Corinthians 13:3 (NRSV)

"Why do I mention the advantages arising from love? Consider for a moment how great a blessing it is in and of itself to exercise love: what cheerfulness it produces, what a great grace it establishes in the soul. Love has the power to shine in us more than anything else. Other virtues each have different troubles yoked with them. Fasting, temperance, and watching, for instance, have envy, lust, and contempt. But love has great pleasure, together with the gain in virtue, and no accompanying trouble. Think of love like an industrious bee, gathering the sweets from every flower and depositing them in the soul of the person who loves." —St. John Chrysostom

I will show love today. Your love will show on my face!

OCTOBER 10

"For [God] has looked upon his handmaid's lowliness;
behold, from now on will all ages call me blessed."
—Luke 1:48 (NAB)

"We arrived in Paris in the morning and immediately began to visit it. [W]e had soon seen all the marvels of the capital. As for me, I found only one that delighted me, and that marvel was Notre-Dame-des-Victoires [Our Lady of Victories, a center of devotion to the Immaculate Heart of Mary]. Oh! What I felt at her feet I wouldn't be able to say. The graces that she granted me moved me so deeply that only my tears betrayed my happiness, as on the day of my first Communion. The Blessed Virgin made me feel that it was truly she who had smiled at me and had healed me. I understood that she was watching over me, that I was her child, so that I could no longer call her anything but Mama, because that name seemed even more tender than that of Mother." —St. Thérèse of Lisieux

Hail Mary. . . .

OCTOBER 11

$\mathcal{L}$et us consider how to stir up one another to love and good works, not neglecting to meet together, as is the habit of some, but encouraging one another, and all the more as you see the Day drawing near.
—Hebrews 10:24–25 (ESV)

"Benedictine spirituality may be defined as living together and getting along with one another. People who do not live in monasteries or have an association with one as oblates might also strive for this same kind of asceticism. A good deal of patience is required in living together whether in a monastery or on the outside. . . . Time is required in the exercise of patience. Some of the characters in a monastery or in an ordinary family live to be very old and their unpleasant characteristics never leave them." —Br. Benet Tvedten, OSB

Where do I need extra patience today?

OCTOBER 12

$\mathcal{I}$ concentrate on doing exactly what you say—
I always have and always will.
—Psalm 119:112 (THE MESSAGE)

"People said that Father John the Dwarf withdrew and lived in the desert with an old man of Thebes. His spiritual guide took a piece of dry wood, planted it, and said to him, 'Water it every day with a bottle of water, until it bears fruit.' Now the water was so far away that he had to leave in the evening and return the following morning. At the end of three years the wood came to life and bore fruit. Then the old man took some of the fruit and carried it to the church, saying to the brothers, 'take and eat the fruit of obedience.'"

—*The Wisdom of the Desert Fathers and Mothers*

Show Me where I am to be obedient today, Lord.

═ OCTOBER 13 ═

*Y*our eyes will see the king in his beauty; they will
behold a land that stretches far away.
—Isaiah 33:17 (NRSV)

"I am not asking you to become involved in long and subtle meditations with your understanding and reason. I am only asking you to look at Christ. Who can prevent you from turning the eyes of your soul upon this Lord? You can look at very ugly things; can't you, then, look at the most beautiful thing imaginable? Your Spouse never takes His eyes off you."

—St. Teresa of Avila

You are beautiful, God.

OCTOBER 14

[Jesus said,] "[I]f I'm telling the truth, why don't you believe
me? Anyone on God's side listens to God's words."
—John 8:46–47a (THE MESSAGE)

"We must not apply our understanding to what is being supernaturally communicated to us, but simply and sincerely apply
our will to God with love. For it is through love that these good
things are communicated, and through love they will be communicated in greater abundance than before."
—St. John of the Cross

God, I'm listening.

OCTOBER 15

Today is the Feast Day of St. Teresa of Avila

"If we keep the vanity of all things constantly in our thoughts,
we will be able to withdraw our affections from trivial things
and fix them on eternal things. This may seem poor advice but
it will fortify the soul greatly. We must be very careful, for as
soon as we begin to grow fond of small things we must withdraw our thoughts from them and turn our thoughts to God.
He has granted us the great favor of providing that, in this
house, most of it is done already. But we must become detached
from ourselves. It is difficult to withdraw from ourselves and
oppose ourselves, because we are very close to ourselves and

love ourselves very dearly. This is where true humility can enter. True humility and detachment from self always go together. You must embrace them, love them, and never be seen without them. . . . The one who possesses them can safely go out and fight all the united forces of hell and the whole world and its temptations. This person does not need to fear anyone, for hers is the kingdom of the heavens. She does not care if she loses everything; her sole fear is that she may displease God, and she begs Him to nourish these virtues within her so she will not lose them through any fault of her own." —St. Teresa of Avila

I want to please You.

═══ OCTOBER 16 ═══

$\mathcal{G}$od doesn't want us to be shy with his gifts,
but bold and loving and sensible.
—2 Timothy 1:7 (THE MESSAGE)

"Some people came one day to test Father John to see whether he would let himself be distracted and speak of the things of this world. They said to him, 'We give thanks to God that this year there has been much rain and the palm trees have been able to drink, and their shoots have grown, and the brothers have found manual work.' Father John said to them, 'So it is when the Holy Spirit descends into the hearts of men; they are renewed and they put forth leaves in the fear of God.'"
—*The Wisdom of the Desert Fathers and Mothers*

I am too easily distracted, Lord. Focus me today.

*B*eloved, we are God's children now; what we will be has not yet been revealed. What we do know is this: when he is revealed, we will be like him, for we will see him as he is.
—1 John 3:2 (NRSV)

"What will it be like when we receive Communion in the everlasting dwelling of the King of heaven? Then we will no longer see our joy come to an end, there will be no more sadness on leaving, and to carry away a souvenir it won't be necessary for us to furtively scratch the walls that have been hallowed by the Divine presence, since His home will be ours for eternity. He doesn't want to give us an earthly home; He's content to show it to us in order to make us love poverty and the hidden life. The home that's reserved for us is His Palace of glory where we'll no longer see Him hidden under the appearance of a Child or a white host, but as He is in the brightness of His infinite splendor!" —St. Thérèse of Lisieux

I look forward to that day to come.

*T*hen I heard every creature in Heaven and earth, in underworld and sea, join in, all voices in all places, singing: To the One on the Throne! To the Lamb! The blessing, the honor, the glory, the strength, for age after age after age.
—Revelation 5:13 (THE MESSAGE)

"No saint better exemplifies the transformative power of one's image of God than Thérèse of Lisieux. Realizing that holiness, in the tradition of the great spiritual giants who had lived before her, was beyond her grasp, she began to practice her 'way of spiritual childhood.' She daily recognized her nothingness, confidently abandoned herself to God, and expected God to give her everything she needed, just as children expect everything from their parents." —Fr. Albert Haase, OFM

Keep teaching me, Your child, O Lord.

OCTOBER 19

Count yourself lucky—GOD holds nothing against you and you're holding nothing back from him. When I kept it all inside, my bones turned to powder, my words became daylong groans. The pressure never let up; all the juices of my life dried up. Then I let it all out; I said, "I'll make a clean breast of my failures to GOD." Suddenly the pressure was gone—my guilt dissolved, my sin disappeared.
—Psalm 32:2–5 (THE MESSAGE)

"Going to confession is hard—hard when you have sins to confess, hard when you haven't, and you rack your brain for even the beginnings of sins against charity, chastity, sins of detraction, sloth or gluttony. . . . 'I have sinned. These are my sins.' That is

all you are supposed to tell; not the sins of others, or your own virtues, but only your ugly, drab, monotonous sins."
—Dorothy Day

**I will remember my sins today, not my virtues,
and not the sins of anyone else.**

═══ OCTOBER 20 ═══

*T*hen he came to the disciples and found them sleeping; and he said to Peter, "So, could you not stay awake with me one hour?"
—Matthew 26:40 (NRSV)

"If you are suffering trials, or are sad, look upon Him on His way to the Garden. What terrible distress He must have carried in His soul, to describe His own suffering as He did and not to complain about it. Or look upon Him on the cross, full of pain, His flesh torn to pieces by His great love for you. How much He suffered: persecuted by some, spit upon by others, denied by His friends with no one to defend Him, frozen with the cold, left completely alone. . . . He looks upon you with His lovely and compassionate eyes, full of tears. In comforting your grief He will forget His own because you are bearing Him company in order to comfort Him and turning your head to look upon Him."
—St. Teresa of Avila

I am here, Lord. I'm not going anywhere.

OCTOBER 21

$\mathcal{G}$OD, investigate my life; get all the facts firsthand. I'm an open book to you; even from a distance, you know what I'm thinking. You know when I leave and when I get back; I'm never out of your sight.
—Psalm 139:1–3 (THE MESSAGE)

"We pray from where we are and not from where we think we should be. There is always a temptation to believe we should be further along in our prayer life, that we shouldn't get bogged down with concerns or worries about our practical, nitty-gritty lives. Consequently we ignore our feelings and often pray around them. In doing so we might try to work ourselves up into an emotional high or find an inner space, attempting to be someone we are not." —Fr. Albert Haase, OFM

Lord, I am praying to You in total honesty. I won't hide anything.

OCTOBER 22

$\mathcal{S}$end forth your bread upon the face of the waters; after a long time you may find it again.
—Ecclesiastes 11:1 (NAB)

"Go on then quickly! Let us see how you carry yourself. Do you not see how He stands and waits for you? For shame! Work eagerly for only a while, and you shall soon be eased of the burden and difficulty of the struggle. For although it is hard and troublesome in the beginning when you have no dedication, nevertheless, after you have dedication to a vow, it shall be made wholly restful and very light for you that before was very hard— and then you shall have either little labor or none at all."

—*The Cloud of Unknowing*

I'm going to keep doing what I'm supposed to do— serving You, honoring You, staying close to You.

═══ OCTOBER 23 ═══

𝒯hat means you must not give sin a vote in the way you conduct your lives. Don't give it the time of day. Don't even run little errands that are connected with that old way of life. Throw yourselves wholeheartedly and full-time—remember, you've been raised from the dead!—into God's way of doing things. Sin can't tell you how to live. After all, you're not living under that old tyranny any longer. You're living in the freedom of God.

—Romans 6:12–14 (The Message)

"At last the devil found he was unable to destroy Antony and that Antony's thoughts were always driving him back. So, crying and gnashing his teeth, he appeared to Antony in a form appropriate to his nature . . . saying in a human voice, 'I have led many astray, and I have deceived many, but you have defeated my efforts, just as other holy people have done.' When Antony asked him who was saying this, the devil replied, 'I am the friend of sin. I have used many different kinds of shameful weapons to attack young people, and that is why I am called the spirit of sinfulness. How many of those who were determined to live chastely have I tricked! How many times have I persuaded those starting out hesitantly to return to their former foul ways. . . . I am the one who has often tempted you, and always you have driven me away.' When the soldier of Christ heard this, he gave thanks to God and, strengthened by greater confidence in the face of the enemy, he said, 'You do not worry me any longer. The Lord is on my side to help me.'"

—*The Wisdom of the Desert Fathers and Mothers*

I will listen to God today, not to my old self.

OCTOBER 24

*C*onsider it a sheer gift, friends, when tests and challenges
come at you from all sides. You know that under pressure,
your faith-life is forced into the open and shows its true colors.
So don't try to get out of anything prematurely.
Let it do its work so you become mature and well-
developed, not deficient in any way.
—James 1:2–4 (THE MESSAGE)

"[Christ] grants miracles and makes mountains move, in order to strengthen [our] faith, which is so tiny. But for His cherished ones, for His Mother, He doesn't do miracles until He has tested their faith. Didn't He let Lazarus die, even though Martha and Mary had told Him that he was sick? At the wedding at Cana, when the Blessed Virgin asked Jesus to help His hosts, didn't He answer her that His hour had not yet come?"

—St. Thérèse of Lisieux [continued tomorrow . . .]

Are You testing me somehow, Lord?

═══ OCTOBER 25 ═══

*J*esus answered and said to him, "Do you believe because I told you . . . ? You will see greater things than this." And he said to him, "Amen, amen, . . . you will see the sky opened and the angels of God ascending and descending on the Son of Man."

—John 1:50–51 (NAB)

[Continued from yesterday] "But after that testing, what a reward! Water changes into wine . . . Lazarus is raised from the dead! That's how Jesus acts toward [me,] His little Thérèse: After testing her for a long time, He fulfills all the desires of her heart."

—St. Thérèse of Lisieux

How will I know You more, once this period of testing is over?

═══ OCTOBER 26 ═══

*T*o this you were called, because Christ suffered for you, leaving you an example, that you should follow in his steps.

—1 Peter 2:21 (NIV)

Meditating on the Cross of Christ, St. Teresa of Avila prayed: "Lord, if You are willing to suffer all this for me, what am I suffering for You? What do I have to complain about? I am ashamed, Lord, when I see You in such a situation. If there is any way I can imitate You I will suffer all trials that come to my way and count them as a great blessing. Lord, let us go together; wherever You go, I must go, and I must pass through whatever You pass."

What do I need to do today?

OCTOBER 27

I was right on the cliff-edge, ready to fall, when God
grabbed and held me. God's my strength, he's
also my song, and now he's my salvation.
—Psalm 118:12–14 (THE MESSAGE)

"Father John said, 'I am like a man sitting under a great tree, who sees wild beasts and snakes coming against him in great numbers. When he cannot withstand them any longer, he runs to climb the tree and is saved. It is just the same with me. I sit in my prayer chamber, and I am aware of evil thoughts coming against me. When I have no more strength against them, I take refuge in God by prayer and I am saved from the enemy.'"
—*The Wisdom of the Desert Fathers and Mothers*

I'm climbing up to You, God.

OCTOBER 28

"The history of the Angelus is obscure, with traces of it stretching back to ninth-century England. It seems most likely, however, that the tolling of the monastery bells calling the monks and nuns to prayer throughout the day, suggested to the ordinary people that they intersperse their daily lives with prayer as well. During the sixteenth century, the tradition emerged of saying the Angelus three times a day, at 6 AM, 12 noon, and 6 PM, often prompted by the tolling of the local church bell."

—Thomas Groome

℣. The angel spoke God's message to Mary,
℟. and she conceived of the Holy Spirit.
   Hail, Mary. . . .

℣. "I am the lowly servant of the Lord:
℟. let it be done to me according to the Your word." Hail, Mary
   . . . .

℣. And the Word became flesh
℟. and lived among us.
   Hail, Mary. . . .

℣. Pray for us, holy Mother of God,
℟. that we may become worthy of the promises of Christ.

$\mathscr{I}$ will stand at my guard post, and station myself upon the
rampart; I will keep watch to see what he will say to me,
and what answer he will give to my complaint.
—Habakkuk 2:1 (NAB)

"The prophet said: I will stand on my watch and set my step on
my tower, and I will watch to see what will be said to me. It is as
if he were to say: I will stand on guard over my faculties and will
take no step forward as to my actions, and so I will be able to
contemplate what will be said to me—that is, I will understand
and enjoy what is communicated to me supernaturally."
—St. John of the Cross

Go to God in prayer. Ask God to speak in the quiet of your soul.

OCTOBER 30

"$\mathscr{S}$uppliant"
by Bonnie Thurston

In the monastery
the note said this:
"pick up your tray
at the kitchen door."

Like how many million
suppliants of ages past,

I am to wait at the portal
for Benedict's brethren
to fill my begging bowl.

I do not know exactly
why this makes me smile,
why I am comforted
to be among the indigent
waiting for crumbs to fall
from the monastic table.

But in history's white light
I see myself as I am,
loitering at heaven's back door
empty-handed and hungry,
waiting with the multitudes
for some disciple
to bless, break and give
God's good bread.

Thank You for the simple things in my life, Lord.

OCTOBER 31

𝒯he fear of God is a paradise of blessings;
its canopy is over all that is glorious.
—Sirach 40:27 (NAB)

"I ask you, by whom shall people's deeds be judged? Surely, by those who have authority and care of their souls, whether that is given publicly by the statute and ordination of Holy Church or else privately and spiritually in perfect charity at the special inspiration of the Holy Spirit. Each person beware lest he presume to take it upon himself to blame and criticize other's faults unless he feels truly that he is inspired by the Holy Spirit as part of his work—for otherwise he can very easily err in his judgments. And therefore beware! Judge yourself as you wish, between you and your God or your spiritual father—but leave other folk alone." —*The Cloud of Unknowing*

I will leave others alone. My own sin is enough for me.

November

NOVEMBER 1

*T*oday is the Feast of All Saints' Day

"Remembering the prayer of Elisha to his father Elijah when he dared to ask for a double portion of his spirit [cf. 2 Kgs. 2:9], I presented myself before the Angels and the Saints, and I told them, 'I am the littlest of creatures, I know my wretchedness and my weakness, but I also know how much noble and generous hearts love to do good. I beg you, then, you Blessed inhabitants of heaven, I beg you to adopt me as your child. To you alone will be the glory that you will cause me to acquire, but deign to grant my prayer. It is foolhardy, I know, but nonetheless I dare to ask you to obtain this for me: a double portion of your Love.'"

—St. Thérèse of Lisieux

What is my prayer today?

NOVEMBER 2

*Y*ou have bid me build a temple on your holy mountain
and an altar in the city that is your dwelling place.
—Wisdom 9:8a (NAB)

"You may say that if you had seen our Lord with your bodily eyes when He was living in the world, you would have gazed at Him forever. Do not believe it. Anyone who will not make the effort to gaze upon this Lord present within her, which she can do with little trouble or danger, would not be likely to have stood at the foot of the cross with St. Mary Magdalene, who looked death straight in the face." —St. Teresa of Avila

**Give me courage, today, Lord, to stand beside You—
even if it makes me feel uncomfortable.**

═══ NOVEMBER 3 ═══

*D*on't run up debts, except for the huge debt of love you owe each other. When you love others, you complete what the law has been after all along. The law code—don't sleep with another person's spouse, don't take someone's life, don't take what isn't yours, don't always be wanting what you don't have, and any other "don't" you can think of—finally adds up to this: Love other people as well as you do yourself. You can't go wrong when you love others. When you add up everything in the law code, the sum total is *love*.
—Romans 13:8–10 (THE MESSAGE)

"Father Moses once said, 'We must die to our neighbors and never judge them at all, in any way whatever.'"
—*The Wisdom of the Desert Fathers and Mothers*

**I know Your commandments, Lord;
I have trouble doing them. Help me.**

NOVEMBER 4

$\mathcal{M}$y dear brothers, take note of this: Everyone should be
quick to listen, slow to speak and slow to become angry.
—James 1:19 (NIV)

"Consider anger. . . . [W]hen love enters in, all the sinews of
anger are taken away from it. Even if he that is beloved should
grieve him who loves him, anger is nowhere to be found; there
are only tears, exhortations, and supplications. Love is very far
from being exasperated." —St. John Chrysostom

**Expose my anger, Lord. Show it to me before it boils.
Help me convert it into love.**

NOVEMBER 5

$\mathcal{S}$o now Israel, what do you think God expects from you?
Just this: Live in his presence in holy reverence, follow the
road he sets out for you, love him, serve God, your God, with
everything you have in you, obey the commandments and
regulations of God that I'm commanding you today—
live a good life.
—Deuteronomy 10:12–13 (THE MESSAGE)

"How sweet is the path of love. No doubt, one can fall down,
one can commit unfaithful acts, but love, knowing how to
profit from everything, quickly consumes everything that can

be displeasing to Jesus, leaving only a humble and profound peace in the depths of the heart." —St. Thérèse of Lisieux

I make mistakes, Lord. Oh my, do I! But I love You. I do.

═══ NOVEMBER 6 ═══

𝒯he last and final word is this: Fear God. Do what he tells you. And that's it. Eventually God will bring everything that we do out into the open and judge it according to its hidden intent, whether it's good or evil.
—Ecclesiastes 12:13–14 (THE MESSAGE)

[When St. Antony knew he was dying] he said to them, "My dear sons, I am going the way of the fathers, to use the words of Scripture. For the Lord is now summoning me, and I long to see heaven. But I warn you who are closest to me not to waste in one moment all the hard work you have put in over a long period. You must think that it is only today that you have started on your life of religious endeavor, and you must allow the strength of your commitment to grow as if it had just begun." —St. Athanasius

I start again, today, Lord, following You.

═══ NOVEMBER 7 ═══

𝒫raise be to the LORD my Rock, who trains my hands for war, my fingers for battle.
—Psalm 144:1 (NIV)

"Father Poemen said of Father John the Dwarf that he had prayed that God would take his passions away from him so that he might become free from care. He went and told an old man this: 'I find myself in peace, without an enemy.' The old man said to him, 'Go, ask God to stir up warfare so that you may regain the affliction and humility that you used to have. For it is by warfare that the soul makes progress.' So he sought God, and when warfare came, he no longer prayed that it might be taken away, but said, 'Lord, give me strength for the fight.'"

—*The Wisdom of the Desert Fathers and Mothers*

Give me strength for the fight, O Christ.

═══ NOVEMBER 8 ═══

[*T*]he sensual man perceiveth not these things that are of the Spirit of God; for it is foolishness to him, and he cannot understand, because it is spiritually examined.

—1 Corinthians 2:14 (Douay-Rheims)

"The logic of worldly success rests on a fallacy: the strange error that our perfection depends on the thoughts and opinions and applause of other men! A weird life it is, indeed, to be living always in somebody else's imagination, as if that were the only place in which one could at last become real!"

—Thomas Merton, OCSO

My reality is in You. This is who I really am.

NOVEMBER 9

[*Jesus said,*] "I'm no longer calling you servants because servants don't understand what their master is thinking and planning. No, I've named you friends because I've let you in on everything I've heard from the Father."
—John 15:15 (THE MESSAGE)

"You will find it very helpful if you can get a picture of the Lord [in your mind] to use regularly when you talk to Him. He will tell you what to say. If you don't have trouble talking to people on earth, why should you have trouble talking to God? Words will not fail you if you form the habit of talking. If you never talk to a person, she soon becomes a stranger and you forget how to talk to her. Before long, even if she is a relative, you will feel like you don't know her. Both family and friends lose their influence when you stop talking to them." —St. Teresa of Avila

I will talk to God, now, as a friend. Or I will just sit quietly, as with a friend.

NOVEMBER 10

The LORD gives strength to his people; the LORD blesses his people with peace.
—Psalm 29:11 (NIV)

"Frustration in prayer is a sign we are trying too hard. Frustration is a good indicator that we are not really praying

from where we are, that perhaps we are being less than honest in our conversation with God. It might also be a sign that we are actively resisting the transformative process initiated by the Spirit of God. In either case, we are trying too hard—to run away from our feelings or to resist God's grace."
—Fr. Albert Haase, OFM

I know that You want me to simply be myself with You.

═══ NOVEMBER 11 ═══

I heard a voice thunder from the Throne: "Look! Look! God has moved into the neighborhood, making his home with men and women! They're his people, he's their God. He'll wipe every tear from their eyes. Death is gone for good—tears gone, crying gone, pain gone—all the first order of things gone." The Enthroned continued, "Look! I'm making everything new. Write it all down—each word dependable and accurate."
—Revelation 21:3–5 (THE MESSAGE)

"Once a priest told us that no one gets up in the pulpit without promulgating a heresy. He was joking, of course, but what I suppose he meant was that the truth was so pure, so holy, that it was hard to emphasize one aspect of the truth without underestimating another, that we did not see things as a whole, but through a glass darkly, as St. Paul said." —Dorothy Day

I look forward to that day, Lord, when I will know You fully.

NOVEMBER 12

*T*here is no health in my flesh, because of thy wrath: there is
no peace for my bones, because of my sins.
—Psalm 37:4 (Douay-Rheims)

"The soul's strength consists in its faculties, passions, and
desires, all of which are governed by the will. When these are
directed by the will toward God and turned away from all that
is not God, the soul's strength is reserved for God. Then the
soul is able to love God with all its strength."
—St. John of the Cross

**There's nothing wrong with my passions and desires,
only with what I sometimes do with them.**

NOVEMBER 13

*Y*our word is a lamp to my feet and a light to my path.
—Psalm 119:105 (esv)

"[A]ll books left me in dryness, and I'm still in that state. If I open
a book written by a spiritual author (even the most beautiful, the
most touching), right away I feel my heart constrict, and I read,
so to speak, without understanding, or if I understand, my mind
stops without being able to meditate. In that state of impotence,
Holy Scripture and the *Imitation of Christ* come to my aid. In
them I find nourishment that is solid and completely pure. But
above all it is the Gospels that keep me fed during my times of

prayer. In them I find everything that is necessary to my poor little soul. In them I always discover new illuminations, hidden and mysterious meanings." —St. Thérèse of Lisieux

Holy Spirit, open Your holy gospel to me. Help me understand.

NOVEMBER 14

" *D*o you think you can explain the mystery of God? Do you think you can diagram God Almighty? God is far higher than you can imagine, far deeper than you can comprehend."
—Job 11:7–8 (THE MESSAGE)

"Think of yourself as only the wood and let it be the carpenter; let yourself be only the house, and let it be the householder dwelling in it. During this time, be blind, and tear away the desire to understand, for that will hinder you more than help you. It is enough for now for you to be lovingly aware of being stirred by something you-know-not-what, so that in your stirring you may have no special thought of anything less than God, and that your intent be nakedly directed to God." —*The Cloud of Unknowing*

Work on me, Christ. You are the master carpenter. I am only wood.

NOVEMBER 15

$\mathcal{D}$o not be deceived; God is not mocked,
for you reap whatever you sow.
—Galatians 6:7 (NRSV)

"We live in a society whose whole policy is to excite every nerve in the human body and keep it at the highest pitch of artificial tension, to strain every human desire to the limit and to create as many new desires and synthetic passions as possible, in order to cater to them with the products of our factories and printing presses and movie studios and all the rest." —Thomas Merton, OCSO

Narrow my focus, Holy Father. I want to see more of Your glory and less of other things.

NOVEMBER 16

[$\mathcal{J}$esus said,] "Here's what I want you to do: Find a quiet, secluded place so you won't be tempted to role-play before God. Just be there as simply and honestly as you can manage. The focus will shift from you to God, and you will begin to sense his grace."
—Matthew 6:6 (THE MESSAGE)

"It might also help to have a good book, written in simple language, to help you in your prayer habits. With such an aid you will learn your vocal prayers well, and little by little your soul will get used to this. Many years have passed since the soul fled from its Spouse, and it needs careful handling before it will return home. We sinners are like that. Our souls and minds are so accustomed to seek their own pleasures until the unfortunate soul no longer knows what it is doing. When that has happened, a good deal of skill is necessary before it can be inspired with enough love to make it stay home. Unless we gradually do this, though, we will not accomplish anything. If you carefully form the kinds of habits I have been writing about, you will gain so much profit from them that I could not describe it even if I wanted to. Stay at this good Master's side, and be determined to learn what He teaches you." —St. Teresa of Avila

I am determined to learn what You want to teach me.

═══ NOVEMBER 17 ═══

*F*or the LORD takes pleasure in his people;
he adorns the humble with victory.
—Psalm 149:4 (NRSV)

"Father John said, 'Who sold Joseph?' A brother replied, 'His brothers.' The old man said to him, 'No, it was his humility that sold him, because he could have said, "I am your brother," and have objected. But, because he kept silence, he sold himself by his humility. It is also his humility that set him up chief in Egypt.' He also said, 'Humility and the fear of God are above all virtues.'"
—*The Wisdom of the Desert Fathers and Mothers*

**I know that I am not humble as I should be, Father.
Does this keep me from You?**

NOVEMBER 18

"Teach me, and I will be silent; make me
understand how I have gone astray."
—Job 6:24 (ESV)

"One of the brothers came to visit and asked him to give him
a valuable teaching. The old man said, 'Go, sit in your room in
solitude, and your room will teach you everything.'"
—*The Wisdom of the Desert Fathers and Mothers*

Sometimes I am afraid of silence. I won't be, today.

NOVEMBER 19

From "Lauds"
by Bonnie Thurston

You are with me,
a gentle embrace
in the alone-ness
of the night.
Your Presence
fills my silent room,
lightens my darkness.

**Remind me of Your presence, Lord, in the smallest,
quietest, simplest of everyday ways.**

NOVEMBER 20

"[*N*]or will they say, 'Look, here it is!' or 'There it is!' For, in fact, the kingdom of God is among you."
—Luke 17:21 (NRSV)

"Jesus has no need of books or teachers to instruct souls. As the Teacher of teachers, He teaches without the noise of words. I have never heard Him speak, but I feel that He is with me. At every moment, He guides me and inspires in me what I ought to say or do. I discover, just at the moment when I need them, understandings that I hadn't yet seen. Most often it's not during my times of prayer that they're the most abundant, but rather in the midst of the occupations of my day." —St. Thérèse of Lisieux

Please speak. I am listening.

NOVEMBER 21

[*D*]idn't you realize that your body is a sacred place, the place of the Holy Spirit? Don't you see that you can't live however you please, squandering what God paid such a high price for? The physical part of you is not some piece of property belonging to the spiritual part of you. God owns the whole works. So let people see God in and through your body.
—1 Corinthians 6:19–20 (THE MESSAGE)

"Body and soul constitute human nature. The body is no less good than the soul. In mortifying the natural we must not injure

the body or the soul. We are not to destroy but to transform it, as iron is transformed in the fire. Most of our life is unimportant, filled with trivial things from morning till night. But when it is transformed by love it is of interest even to the angels."
—Dorothy Day

I will use my body today in service to God.

═ NOVEMBER 22 ═

$\mathcal{G}$OD, my shepherd! I don't need a thing. Your beauty
and love chase after me every day of my life.
—Psalm 23:1, 6a (THE MESSAGE)

"First of all, you have to keep unmasking the world about you for what it is: manipulative, controlling, power-hungry, and, in the long run, destructive. The world tells you many lies about who you are, and you simply have to be realistic enough to remind yourself of this. Every time you feel hurt, offended, or rejected, you have to dare to say to yourself: 'These feelings, strong as they may be, are not telling me the truth about myself. The truth, even though I cannot feel it right now, is that I am the chosen child of God, precious in God's eyes, called the Beloved from all eternity, and held safe in an everlasting belief.'" —Henri J. M. Nouwen

I am Yours; and in You, I know who I am.

[*Jesus said,*] "Thus therefore shall you pray: Our Father
who art in heaven, hallowed be thy name."
—Matthew 6:9 (Douay-Rheims)

"My Lord, how fittingly You reveal Yourself as the father of such
a Son. How fittingly Your Son reveals Himself as the Son of such
a Father. May You be blessed forever and ever. Shouldn't a favor
as great as this one come at the end of the prayer? Here at the
beginning You fill our hands and grant us so great a favor that
it would be a great blessing if our understanding could be filled
and our will occupied. We would thus be unable to say another
word. How appropriate perfect contemplation would be here.
How right the soul would be to enter into itself, so it could rise
above itself and so that this holy Son might show it the nature of
the place where He says his Father dwells—in the heavens. Let us
leave earth, for it is not right that such a favor should be valued
so little." —St. Teresa of Avila

Our Father. . . .

$\mathcal{B}$ut all who are hunting for you—oh, let them sing and be happy. Let those who know what you're all about tell the world you're great and not quitting. And me? I'm a mess. I'm nothing and have nothing: make something of me. You can do it; you've got what it takes—but God, don't put it off.

—Psalm 40:16–17 (THE MESSAGE)

"It is a kind of pride to insist that none of our prayers should ever be petitions for our own needs: for this is only another subtle way of trying to put ourselves on the same plane as God—acting as if we had no needs, as if we were not creatures, not dependent on Him and dependent, by His will, on material things, too."
—Thomas Merton OCSO

**I have so many needs, Lord, that sometimes
I don't know what to do.**

$\mathcal{T}$he Spirit helps us in our weakness. We do not know what we ought to pray for, but the Spirit himself intercedes for us through wordless groans.

—Romans 8:26 (NIV)

"If [your prayer] is only a word of one syllable, I would consider it better than two, and more in accord with the work of the Spirit since it is thus that a spiritual laborer in this Work should always be in the highest and most supreme place of the spirit. That this is true, see by example of the course of nature: a man or a woman, fearful of any sudden risk of fire, or of one's death, or whatever else may be, suddenly in the intensity of one's spirit is driven to rush and to the need to cry out or to pray for help. . . . Surely not in many words nor even in a word of two syllables. And why? Because he thinks it would be waiting too long to declare the need and the affliction of his spirit. And therefore he bursts out shockingly with great feeling, and cries out only a little word of one syllable, like the word 'Fire!'" —*The Cloud of Unknowing*

God—what can I say? Help!

═══ NOVEMBER 26 ═══

$\mathcal{D}$o not love the world or anything in the world. If anyone loves the world, love for the Father is not in them.
—1 John 2:15 (NIV)

"There are many nowadays whose reason is darkened to spiritual things by greed. They serve money and not God and are influenced by money and not by God. They put the cost of a thing first, and not its divine worth and reward, and in many ways make money their principal god and end, and place it ahead of the final end, which is God." —St. John of the Cross

As this Advent approaches, Holy Spirit, examine my heart. If I am loving the wrong things, show me.

NOVEMBER 27

$\mathcal{I}$ am GOD, the only God there is. Besides me there are no real gods. I'm the one who armed you for this work, though you don't even know me.
—Isaiah 45:5 (THE MESSAGE)

"What sweet joy it is to think that God is just—that is, that He takes into account our weakness, He knows perfectly the fragility of our nature. What should I be afraid of? Oh! The infinitely just God who deigned to forgive with such kindness all the faults of the prodigal son, should He not also be just toward me?"
—St. Thérèse of Lisieux

I am grateful for Your grace today.

NOVEMBER 28

$\mathcal{M}$y child, if you accept my words . . . making your ear attentive to wisdom and inclining your heart to understanding . . . then you will understand the fear of the LORD and find the knowledge of God.
—Proverbs 2:1, 2, 5 (NRSV)

"People said that Father John went to church one day and he heard some brothers arguing. So he returned to his prayer chamber. He went round it three times and then went in. Some

people who had seen him, wondered why he had done this. They went and asked him. He said to them, 'My ears were full of that argument, so I circled round in order to purify them, and thus I entered my prayer chamber with my mind at rest.'"
—*The Wisdom of the Desert Fathers and Mothers*

I will guard my ears today, Lord.

═ NOVEMBER 29 ═

*D*orothy Day died on this day in 1980.

"We cannot love God unless we love each other, and to love we must know each other. We know Him in the breaking of bread, and we know each other in the breaking of bread, and we are not alone any more. Heaven is a banquet and life is a banquet, too, even with a crust, where there is companionship."
—Dorothy Day

**Dear Christ, deepen my love and relationships
with friends and family today.**

*L*ong before he laid down earth's foundations, he had us in mind, had settled on us as the focus of his love, to be made whole and holy by his love. Long, long ago he decided to adopt us into his family through Jesus Christ.

—Ephesians 1:4–5a (THE MESSAGE)

"We may be little, insignificant servants in the eyes of a world motivated by efficiency, control, and success. But when we realize that God has chosen us from all eternity, sent us into the world as the blessed ones, handed us over to suffering, can't we, then, also trust that our little lives will multiply themselves and be able to fulfill the needs of countless people?" —Henri J. M. Nouwen

**I can't fathom You knowing and loving me,
yet I know that You do!**

December

═══ DECEMBER 1 ═══

"*K*now that I am with you and will keep you wherever you go, and will bring you back to this land; for I will not leave you until I have done what I have promised you."
—Genesis 28:15 (NRSV)

"You know that God is everywhere. This is a great truth, for wherever God is, there is heaven. You can believe that in any place where our Lord resides, there is fullness of glory. Recall that St. Augustine tells us about his seeking God in many places and eventually finding Him within Himself. A soul that is often distracted needs to understand this truth, for in order to speak to its Eternal Father and to take its delight in Him, it has no need to go to heaven or to speak in a loud voice. No matter how quietly we speak, He is so near that He will hear us."
—St. Teresa of Avila [continued tomorrow . . .]

No matter how "low" I go, You're there. Thank You for that.

═══ DECEMBER 2 ═══

*W*hen you search for me, you will find me; if you seek me with all your heart.
—Jeremiah 29:13 (NRSV)

[St. Teresa of Avila continues,] "We do not need wings to search for Him. We need only to find a place where we can be alone and look upon Him present within us. We don't need to feel strange in the presence of such a kind Guest. We must talk very humbly to Him, as we should to our father, ask Him for things as we should ask a father, tell Him our troubles, beg Him to correct them, and realize that we are not worthy to be called His children."

—St. Teresa of Avila [continued tomorrow . . .]

I can't fathom You, but I know You made me in Your image.

══ DECEMBER 3 ══

$\mathscr{P}$raise the LORD, MY SOUL; all my inmost being,
praise his holy name.
—Psalm 103:1 (NIV)

[Sr. Teresa of Avila continues,] "Speak to God as with a Father, a Brother, a Lord, and a Spouse. He will teach you what you need to do to please Him. Do not be foolish. Ask Him to let you speak to Him. Remember how important it is to understand that the Lord is within us and that we should be there with Him. If you pray in this way, the prayer may be only vocal, but the mind will enter into the prayer much sooner. This is a prayer that brings a thousand blessings with it. It is called recollection because the soul collects all the faculties together and enters within itself to be with its God. Its Divine Master comes more speedily to teach it and to grant it the Prayer of Quiet."

I want to tell You things, but I also want to sit quietly in Your presence without talking.

DECEMBER 4

Teresa and John
by Br. Paul Quenon, OCSO

Nuns of Avila misunderstood
and reported that Teresa and John,
in conversation about things eternal,
had levitated above their chairs.

But their perception had gone askew.

For the two, steadied in Love Unmoveable,
had remained fixed, and the chairs, the room,
and the turning world had dropped aslant,
as they're wont to do.

Help me stay focused on You, Lord—and not on the world.

DECEMBER 5

*Love is patient; love is kind; love is not envious
or boastful or arrogant.*
—1 Corinthians 13:4 (NRSV)

"Don't pass hastily by the things he has spoken, my friends, but
examine each one of them with care, so that you may know
the treasure that is in the thing as well as the art of the painter
himself. Consider, for example, his point of departure—what
Paul proposes as the cause of all of love's excellence. What is it?

Patience. Patience is the root of all self-denial. In this regard, a wise man once said, 'Whoever is slow to anger has great understanding, but one who has a hasty temper exalts folly' (Prov. 14:29)." —St. John Chrysostom

Bless me with greater patience today, Lord.
You know where I need it.

*O*n your feet now—applaud GOD! Bring a gift of laughter,
sing yourselves into his presence. Know this: GOD is God,
and God, GOD. He made us; we didn't make him.
We're his people, his well-tended sheep.
—Psalm 100:1–3 (THE MESSAGE)

"Oh, my Jesus! To all my foolishness, what are You going to reply?" —St. Thérèse of Lisieux

Thank You for taking me just as I am, foolish and all.

[*J*esus said,] "Then the King will say to those on his right, 'Come, you who are blessed by my Father, inherit the kingdom prepared for you from the foundation of the world. For I was hungry and you gave me food, I was thirsty and you gave me drink, I was a stranger and you welcomed me, I was naked and

you clothed me, I was sick and you visited me,
I was in prison and you came to me.'"
—Matthew 25:34–36 (ESV)

"Father John the Dwarf said, 'A house is not built by beginning at the top and working down. You must begin with the foundations in order to reach the top.' They said to him, 'What does this saying mean?' He said, 'The foundation is our neighbor, whom we must win, and that is the place to begin. For all the commandments of Christ depend on this one.'"
—*The Wisdom of the Desert Fathers and Mothers*

Show me a new way to love my neighbor today, Lord.

DECEMBER 8

[*I*]f any of you lacks wisdom, he should ask God who gives to all generously and ungrudgingly, and he will be given it.
—James 1:5 (NAB)

"St. Anselm, a Benedictine monk and theologian of the early twelfth century, explained the purpose of theology with the now-famous phrase: *fides quaerens intellectum*, 'faith seeking understanding.' In other words, theology stands upon a foundation of faith and reaches outward for greater understanding which helps faith to grow. Without it, we are stagnant. St. Augustine wrote something similar when he cried out in his *Confessions*: 'Let me seek Thee, Lord . . . and let me utter my prayer believing in Thee. . . . My faith, Lord, cries to Thee, the faith that Thou hast given me.'" —Fr. Thomas J. Scirghi, SJ

Help me understand. My faith still seeks to know more.

═══ DECEMBER 9 ═══

𝒞onsider it a sheer gift, friends, when tests and challenges come at you from all sides. You know that under pressure, your faith-life is forced into the open and shows its true colors. So don't try to get out of anything prematurely. Let it do its work so you become mature and well-developed, not deficient in any way.
—James 1:2–4 (The Message)

"The more you try to avoid suffering, the more you suffer, because smaller and more insignificant things begin to torture you, in proportion to your fear of being hurt. The one who does most to avoid suffering is, in the end, the one who suffers most."
—Thomas Merton, OCSO

Everyday life I can handle, God. A moment distant from You, I can't.

DECEMBER 10

$\mathcal{D}$avid also commanded the chiefs of the Levites to appoint
their kindred as the singers to play on musical instruments, on
harps and lyres and cymbals, to raise loud sounds of joy.
—1 Chronicles 15:16 (NRSV)

"The spiritual person rejoices in all things—since his joy is
dependent on none of them—as if he had them all."
—St. John of the Cross

The things that give me joy are from You.

DECEMBER 11

$\mathcal{Y}$ou are Christ's body—that's who you are! You must
never forget this. Only as you accept your part of
that body does your "part" mean anything.
—1 Corinthians 12:27 (THE MESSAGE)

"I have found my place in the Church, and that place, my God,
You have given me. In the Heart of the Church . . . I will be Love."
—St. Thérèse of Lisieux

I will try and show Christ's love to the people around me today.

*B*e good to me, God—and now! I've run to you for dear life.
I'm hiding out under your wings until the hurricane blows
over. I call out to High God, the God who holds me together.
—Psalm 57:1–2 (THE MESSAGE)

"[W]hy does [a prayer of one word or syllable] pierce heaven . . .?
Certainly because it is prayed with a full spirit, in the height and
in the depth, in the length and in the breadth of the spirit of the
one who prays it. It is in the height—for it is with all the power of
the spirit; it is in the depths—for in this little syllable is contained
all the wisdom of the spirit; it is in the length—for if it were to
feel over a stretch of time as it feels at the moment, it would cry
then just as it cries now; it is in the breadth—for it desires for all
others what it desires for itself. In this moment it is that a soul
has grasped . . . what is the length and the breadth, the height
and the depths of the Everlasting and All-loving Almighty and
All-wise God." —*The Cloud of Unknowing*

Are You listening, God? Please hear my cry.

DECEMBER 13

*I*n the beginning was the Word, and the Word was
with God, and the Word was God.
—John 1:1 (NAB)

"You might recall the stories in the Gospels where Jesus restores sight to the blind. For example, you may recall the story of the blind man Bartimaeus (cf. Mk. 10:46–52). He used to sit along the roadside which led to the city of Jericho, begging. One day Jesus and his disciples happened to be passing by with a crowd surrounding them. Bartimaeus sensed the Lord's presence and shouted to Him, 'Son of David, have pity on me!' Jesus halted in His tracks and His disciples brought the man to Him. Bartimaeus stood before Jesus and pleaded, 'Master, let me receive my sight.' Jesus responded, 'Go your way, your faith has made you well.' Immediately the man could see and he followed Jesus. In a sense Jesus's whole mission on earth could be thought of as just that—restoring sight to humanity.

However, the beginning of John's Gospel is not about a divine ability to restore physical sight. Rather, it is about insight, the cultivation of deeper understanding. When we gain insight, available from God alone, then the way in which we understand creation changes because, through the light of Christ, the world is given new meaning. This new meaning occurs when we stand in a new relationship with God. The sacraments of the church provide a glimpse of spiritual insight, enabling us to recognize the presence of the Lord in our midst and to respond to His call."
—Fr. Thomas J. Scirghi, SJ

Restore my sight, Lord. I am so blind.

DECEMBER 14

$\mathcal{G}$od gives some people wealth, possessions and honor,
so that they lack nothing their hearts desire, but God
does not grant them the ability to enjoy them,
and strangers enjoy them instead. . . .
—Ecclesiastes 6:2 (NIV)

"Father Isidore of Pelusia said, 'The desire for possessions is dangerous and terrible, knowing no satiety; it drives the soul that it controls to the heights of evil. Therefore, let us drive it away vigorously from the beginning. For once it has become master, it cannot be overcome.'"
—*The Wisdom of the Desert Fathers and Mothers*

I want less and less of the world, Lord, and more and more of You.

DECEMBER 15

$\mathcal{B}$ut I have calmed and quieted myself, I am like a weaned
child with its mother; like a weaned child I am content.
—Psalm 131:2 (NIV)

"Those Christians who are able to shut themselves up in this little heaven of the soul, wherein the Maker of heaven and earth dwells, and who have formed the habit of looking at nothing and staying in no place that distracts the senses, may be sure that they are walking on an excellent road. They will not fail to drink of the water of the fountain, for they will travel a long way in a

short time. They are like travelers on a ship who, with a little good wind, reach the end of their voyage in a few days, while those who travel by land take much longer to arrive."
—St. Teresa of Avila

If I am quiet, will you talk to me?

═══ DECEMBER 16 ═══

*H*appy are those who do not follow the advice of the wicked, or take the path that sinners tread, or sit in the seat of scoffers; but their delight is in the law of the LORD, and on his law they meditate day and night.
—Psalm 1:1–2 (NRSV)

"Father Moses said, 'Bear your own faults and do not pay attention to anyone else, wondering whether they are good or bad. Do not harm anyone; do not harbor evil thoughts in your heart toward anyone; do not condemn the person who commits evil; do not have confidence in the person who does wrong to his neighbor; do not rejoice with the one who injures his neighbor. Do not agree with the one who slanders his neighbor, and do not hate the one who slanders his neighbor. This is what it means not to judge. Do not harbor hostile feelings toward anyone, and do not let malice dominate your heart. This is what peace is.'"
—*The Wisdom of the Desert Fathers and Mothers*

**I know it isn't enough that I follow Your commandments.
I should help others follow them too.**

DECEMBER 17

[W]e have three things to do . . . : Trust steadily in God,
hope unswervingly, love extravagantly
And the best of the three is love.
—1 Corinthians 13:13b (THE MESSAGE)

"A Christian must rejoice, not in performing good works and
following good customs, but in doing them for the love of God
alone, without respect to anything else whatsoever. Seeing that
only good works that are done to serve God will have the greater
reward in glory, the greater will be the confusion in the presence
of God of those who have done them for other reasons."
—St. John of the Cross

**I help others not to "look good," but to be who
I'm supposed to be.**

DECEMBER 18

O God, from my youth you have taught me, and I still
proclaim your wondrous deeds.
—Psalm 71:17 (NRSV)

"How can a soul as imperfect as mine aspire to possess the fullness of Love? Jesus! My first, my only Friend, You whom ALONE
I love, tell me, what is this mystery? Why do You not reserve
these immense aspirations to great souls, to the eagles that soar
in the heights? I consider myself as a weak little bird covered

only with a light down. I am not an eagle, I simply have an eagle's eyes and heart." —St. Thérèse of Lisieux

I want to soar, Lord! Bless me, so that I may know You at great heights!

═ DECEMBER 19 ═

"Lead, Kindly Light, amid th'encircling gloom,
    Lead Thou me on!
The night is dark, and I am far from home—
    Lead Thou me on!
Keep Thou my feet; I do not ask to see
The distant scene; one step enough for me."

—Blessed John Henry, Cardinal Newman

Please fill my life with Your holy light, today, and during this holy season, O Lord.

═ DECEMBER 20 ═

God—you're my God! I can't get enough of you!
I've worked up such hunger and thirst for God,
    traveling across dry and weary deserts.
        —Psalm 63:1 (THE MESSAGE)

"The brothers also asked Father Agathon, 'Which virtue requires the greatest effort among all the good works?' He answered, 'Forgive me, but I think there is no labor greater than prayer to God. For every time a man wants to pray, his enemies, the demons, want to prevent him. For they know that it is only by turning him from prayer that they can hinder his journey. Whatever good work a man undertakes, if he perseveres in it, he will attain rest. But prayer is warfare to the last breath.'"

—*The Wisdom of the Desert Fathers and Mothers*

My prayers sustain me because that's when I'm most connected to You.

═══ DECEMBER 21 ═══

I've always longed to live in a place like this, always
dreamed of a room in your house, where I could sing
for joy to God-alive!
—Psalm 84:1b–2 (THE MESSAGE)

"God initiates the process of spiritual transformation by throwing a divine spark into our lives. God then waits for our response." —Fr. Albert Haase, OFM

What sparks are You throwing my way, Lord? Guide me, Holy Spirit, so that I know how to kindle them!

For a day in your courts is better than a thousand elsewhere. I would rather be a doorkeeper in the house of my God than live in the tents of wickedness.

—Psalm 84:10 (NRSV)

"Let us imagine that we have within us a palace built of gold and precious stones fit for so great a Lord. Imagine that you are partially responsible for the beauty of the palace. There is no building so beautiful as a soul that is pure and full of virtues; the greater these virtues are, the more brilliantly the stones shine. Imagine that within the palace dwells this great King, who has come down to be your Father, and who sits upon a throne of supreme price—your heart." —St. Teresa of Avila

I will decorate the walls of my palace (wherever I am) with prayers of praise to You.

DECEMBER 23

Stay on good terms with each other, held together by love. Be ready with a meal or a bed when it's needed. Why, some have extended hospitality to angels without ever knowing it! Regard prisoners as if you were in prison with them. Look on victims of abuse as if what happened to them had happened to you.

—Hebrews 13:1–3 (THE MESSAGE)

"Father Agathon once said, 'Even if a person raises the dead but is full of anger, that person is not acceptable to God.' Going to town one day to sell some small articles, on the roadside Agathon met a cripple, who asked him where he was going. Agathon replied, 'To town, to sell some things.' The other said, 'Please carry me there with you.' So he carried him to the town. The cripple said to him, 'Put me down where you sell your wares.' Agathon did so. When he had sold an article, the cripple asked, 'What did you sell it for?' And he told him the price. The other said, 'Buy me a cake,' and he bought it. When Agathon had sold a second article, the sick man asked, 'How much did you sell it for?' And he told him the price of it. Then the other said, 'Buy me this,' and he bought it. When Agathon, having sold all his wares, wanted to go, the sick man said to him, 'Are you going back?' and he replied, 'Yes.' Then the paralyzed man said, 'Please carry me back to the place where you found me.' Once more picking him up, Agathon carried him back to that place. Then the cripple said, 'Agathon, you are filled with divine blessings, in heaven and on earth.' Raising his eyes, Agathon saw no man; it was an angel of the Lord, come to try him."

—*The Wisdom of the Desert Fathers and Mothers*

Give me the perseverance to make my life beautiful for You.

DECEMBER 24

It is he alone who has immortality and dwells in unapproachable light, whom no one has ever seen or can see; to him be honor and eternal dominion. Amen.
—1 Timothy 6:16 (NRSV)

"O Divine Word, You are the adored Eagle whom I love and who draws me. You are the One who, launching out to this world of exile, was willing to suffer and die in order to draw souls to the midst of the Eternal Home of the Blessed Trinity. It is You, going back up toward the unapproachable Light that will henceforth be Your dwelling place; it is You still remaining in the valley of tears, hidden under the appearance of a white host. Everlasting Eagle, You want to feed me with Your divine Substance, I, poor little being, who would return back into nothingness if Your divine gaze were not giving me life at each moment. Oh, Jesus!"
—St. Thérèse of Lisieux

I am making room for You in my life and home, tonight.

DECEMBER 25

"The House of Christmas"
by G. K. Chesterton

"There fared a mother driven forth
Out of an inn to roam;
In the place where she was homeless

All men are at home.
The crazy stable close at hand,
With shaking timber and shifting sand,
Grew a stronger thing to abide and stand
Than the square stones of Rome.

For men are homesick in their homes,
And strangers under the sun,
And they lay their heads in a foreign land
Whenever the day is done.
Here we have battle and blazing eyes,
And chance and honor and high surprise,
But our homes are under miraculous skies
Where the yule tale was begun.

A Child in a foul stable,
Where the beasts feed and foam;
Only where He was homeless
Are you and I at home;
We have hands that fashion and heads that know,
But our hearts we lost—how long ago!
In a place no chart nor ship can show
Under the sky's dome.

This world is wild as an old wives' tale,
And strange the plain things are,
The earth is enough and the air is enough
For our wonder and our war;
But our rest is as far as the fire-drake swings
And our peace is put in impossible things

Where clashed and thundered unthinkable wings
Round an incredible star.

To an open house in the evening
Home shall men come,
To an older place than Eden
And a taller town than Rome.
To the end of the way of the wandering star,
To the things that cannot be and that are,
To the place where God was homeless
And all men are at home."

**Bless my home, today, Lord, even as I'm reminded
that You are my true home.**

Today is the Feast Day of St. Stephen,
the first Christian martyr

"Look," [Stephen] said, "I see the heavens opened and the Son of Man standing at the right hand of God!" —Acts 7:56 (NRSV)

"There is a 'Word' that may be used to describe man's prayerful contemplation of God, and it is Christ Himself, perfect expression of the Father. It is no accident that the first Christian mystical experience, the vision vouchsafed the deacon Stephen as he gave his life for Christ, bears the imprint of this 'Word' that Christ is. . . . But that word, that name, was intolerable to

Stephen's persecutors, who 'shouted out and stopped their ears with their hands' as they killed the man who pronounced it (Acts 7:57). . . . [S]imply to pronounce the name 'Jesus Christ' constitutes prayer, and various ecclesial traditions invite believers to the mantra-like repetition of this name by which sinful humankind is saved." —Timothy Verdon

Jesus Christ, to You I pray. Jesus. Jesus. Jesus.

═ DECEMBER 27 ═

To the King of the ages, immortal, invisible, the only God, be honor and glory forever and ever. Amen.
—1 Timothy 1:17 (NRSV)

"The truly devout person sets his devotion principally on what is invisible. He needs few images and uses few, and chooses those that harmonize with the Divine rather than with the human, clothing them, and with them himself, in the garments of the world to come, and following its fashions rather than those of this world." —St. John of the Cross

I don't need to see You, and I don't need to touch You, to praise You.

DECEMBER 28

$\mathcal{A}$ new heart I will give you, and a new spirit I will put within you; and I will remove from your body the heart of stone and give you a heart of flesh.

—Ezekiel 36:26 (NRSV)

Father Poemen said, "These three things are the most helpful of all: fear of the Lord, prayer, and doing good to one's neighbor."

"A person who stays in his place in life will not be troubled."

"Teach your heart to guard what your tongue teaches."

"If a man understands something and does not practice it, how can he teach it to his neighbor?"

"Not understanding what has happened prevents us from going on to something better."

"Do not lay open your conscience to anyone whom you do not trust in your heart."

—*The Wisdom of the Desert Fathers and Mothers*

Amen.

DECEMBER 29

$\mathcal{B}$lessed be the LORD, the God of Israel, from everlasting and to everlasting. And let all the people say, "Amen!" Praise the LORD.

—Psalm 106:48 (NRSV)

"Those of you who cannot focus your constantly wandering thoughts on God must at all costs form this habit. I know you are capable of it. I also know that the Lord will help you if you approach Him humbly and ask Him to be with you. If an entire year passes without your obtaining what you ask for, you should be prepared to continue asking. You should never complain about time so well spent. It is possible to form the habit of walking at this true Master's side." —St. Teresa of Avila

When in doubt, I will praise You.

=== **DECEMBER 30** ===

$\mathcal{M}$y heart is steadfast, O God, my heart is steadfast.
I will sing and make melody.
—Psalm 57:7 (NRSV)

"Although churches and pleasant places are set apart and furnished for prayer (for a church must not be used for anything else), for a matter as intimate as conversing with God one should choose a place that gives the senses the least occupation and the least encouragement. This is why Our Savior chose solitary places for prayer. He chose places that lift up the soul to God, such as mountains, which are lifted up above the earth and are usually bare, offering no occasion for exercising the senses."
—St. John of the Cross

I want only You, Lord God, wherever I may be.

DECEMBER 31

*Evening, morning and noon I cry out in distress,
and he hears my voice.*
—Psalm 55:17 (NIV)

"There are only two ceremonies that He taught us to use in our prayers: we are to pray in the secret place of our chamber, where without noise and without paying attention to anyone we can pray with the most perfect and pure heart. He said: When you pray, enter into your chamber and shut the door and pray. Or else He taught us to go to a solitary and desert place, as He Himself did, and at the best and quietest time of night." —St. John of the Cross

**I commit myself again, at the start of another year,
to spend time each day with You.**

$\mathcal{S}$ources

Unless noted, all sources are published by Paraclete Press, Inc., www.paracletepress.com

St. Athanasius, *The Life of St. Antony*, from *The Wisdom of the Desert Fathers and Mothers*.

Br. Benet Tvedten, OSB, *How to Be a Monastic and Not Leave Your Day Job*.

Enzo Bianchi, *Echoes of the Word*.

St. Catherine of Siena, *Little Talks with God*.

G. K. Chesterton, *Saint Francis of Assisi*.

The Complete Cloud of Unknowing, trans. by Fr. John-Julian, OJN.

Desert Fathers and Mothers, in *The Wisdom of the Desert Fathers and Mothers*.

Dorothy Day, *The Long Loneliness*.

St. Francis of Assisi, from *Francis of Assisi in His Own Words: The Essential Writings*, trans. and annotated by Jon M. Sweeney.

Thomas Groome (ed. with Colleen Griffith), *Catholic Spiritual Practices*.

Fr. Albert Haase, OFM. *Catching Fire, Becoming Flame*.

Sr. Bridget Haase, OSU, *Doors to the Sacred*.

St. John Chrysostom, *The Love Chapter: The Meaning of First Corinthians 13*.

St. John of the Cross, *Ascent of Mount Carmel*.

Thomas Merton, OCSO, *The Seven Storey Mountain* (New York: Harcourt Brace, 1999).

Henri J. M. Nouwen, *Life of the Beloved: Spiritual Living in a Secular World* (New York: Crossroad, 2002).

Br. Paul Quenon, OCSO, *Unquiet Vigil: New and Selected Poems*.

Fr. Thomas J. Scirghi, SJ, *Everything Is Sacred: A Complete Introduction to the Sacrament of Baptism*.

St. Teresa of Avila. *The Way of Perfection*.

Bonnie Thurston, *Practicing Silence: New and Selected Verses*.

Timothy Verdon. *Art & Prayer: A Celebration of Turning to God*.

About Paraclete Press

WHO WE ARE

Paraclete Press is a publisher of books, recordings, and DVDs on Christian spirituality. Our publishing represents a full expression of Christian belief and practice—from Catholic to Evangelical, from Protestant to Orthodox.

We are the publishing arm of the Community of Jesus, an ecumenical monastic community in the Benedictine tradition. As such, we are uniquely positioned in the marketplace without connection to a large corporation and with informal relationships to many branches and denominations of faith.

WHAT WE ARE DOING

PARACLETE PRESS BOOKS | Paraclete publishes books that show the richness and depth of what it means to be Christian. Although Benedictine spirituality is at the heart of all that we do, we publish books that reflect the Christian experience across many cultures, time periods, and houses of worship. We publish books that nourish the vibrant life of the church and its people.

We have several different series, including the best-selling Paraclete Essentials and Paraclete Giants series of classic texts in contemporary English; Voices from the Monastery—men and women monastics writing about living a spiritual life today; award-winning poetry; best-selling gift books for children on the occasions of baptism and first communion; and the Active Prayer Series that brings creativity and liveliness to any life of prayer.

MOUNT TABOR BOOKS | Paraclete's newest series, Mount Tabor Books, focuses on liturgical worship, art and art history, ecumenism, and the first millennium church; and was created in conjunction with the Mount Tabor Ecumenical Centre for Art and Spirituality in Barga, Italy.

PARACLETE RECORDINGS | From Gregorian chant to contemporary American choral works, our recordings celebrate the best of sacred choral music composed through the centuries that create a space for heaven and earth to intersect. Paraclete Recordings is the record label representing the internationally acclaimed choir Gloriæ Dei Cantores, praised for their "rapt and fathomless spiritual intensity" by American Record Guide; the Gloriæ Dei Cantores Schola, specializing in the study and performance of Gregorian chant; and the other instrumental artists of the Gloriæ Dei Artes Foundation.

Paraclete Press is also privileged to be the exclusive North American distributor of the recordings of the Monastic Choir of St. Peter's Abbey in Solesmes, France, long considered to be a leading authority on Gregorian chant.

PARACLETE VIDEO | Our DVDs offer spiritual help, healing, and biblical guidance for a broad range of life issues including grief and loss, marriage, forgiveness, facing death, bullying, addictions, Alzheimer's, and spiritual formation.

Learn more about us at our website:
www.paracletepress.com or
phone us toll-free at 1.800.451.5006

SCAN TO READ MORE

You may also be interested in . . .

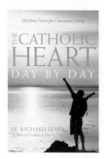

The Catholic Heart Day by Day
Uplifting Stories for Courageous Living
Fr. Richard Beyer
ISBN: 978-1-55725-600-3 | $16.95, Paperback

The Catholic Heart is about the living love, trust in God, and heroism of everyday Christians. These stories of faith and courage will find their way into your heart each morning. They have the power to slowly transform your life over the course of the next year.

Freedom and Forgiveness
A Fresh Look at the Sacrament of Reconciliation
Father Paul Farren
Foreword by Jean Vanier
ISBN: 978-1-61261-498-4 | $8.99, Paperback

"Somewhere, along the line, in the history of the Church, people have become more centered upon obedience to laws than upon this relationship with love with a person, with Jesus. This book flows from an understanding of Confession as a meeting of love and as a renewal of friendship." —Jean Vanier, from the foreword

Catching Fire, Becoming Flame
A Guide for Spiritual Transformation
Albert Haase, OFM

ISBN: 978-1-61261-297-3 | $16.99, Paperback

Albert Haase gives the tools and kindling to prepare for the spark of God in your life—and shows how to fan it into flame. This book glows with time-tested wisdom as an experienced spiritual director shares the secrets of the saints. This eminently practical book functions like a personal spiritual retreat.

Available from most booksellers or through Paraclete Press:
www.paracletepress.com
1-800-451-5006
Try your local bookstore first.